CHOOSE FREEDOM — THE JOURNEY

By
Don L. Sutton

Amy: Thank you for sharing your family with me. I love you all.
Don

PublishAmerica
Baltimore

© 2005 by Don L. Sutton
All rights reserved. No part of this book may be reproduced, stored in a retrieval system or transmitted in any form or by any means without the prior written permission of the publishers, except by a reviewer who may quote brief passages in a review to be printed in a newspaper, magazine or journal.

First printing

Cover art idea from the author's son, Robert.

ISBN: 1-4137-8379-1
PUBLISHED BY PUBLISHAMERICA, LLLP
www.publishamerica.com
Baltimore

Printed in the United States of America

To My Sarah,
We Miss You.

And to you, Matthew Janik, thank you for all the technical help and support. Without you, it could have taken me another four years to complete this task.
I Love You, Bro!

My name is Don L. Sutton; I am 55 years young and wrinkled. I was born in Portland, Oregon, on October 21, 1949. I have two brothers, Dennis and Michael; one sister, Deborah; one half-brother; one stepbrother; and two stepsisters. My mother passed away Christmas Eve 1979, and my father, Charles, is 82 years old.

I have been clean and sober for over 18 glorious years. I walked into a treatment center on August 6, 1989, and walked out a different person, 33 days later.

I have been married to my Peggy for over 36 years. We have a son, Robert, 35 years old, and a daughter, Rebecca, 33 years old. Both children are married, and Rebecca gave me a grandson, Anthony, who is 10 years old. A grandson, Samuel, and a granddaughter, Olivia, were given to me by Robert. Wayne is my son-in-law, and Kimberly is my daughter-in-law. Peggy and I met in 1960. We started dating in 1965 during high school and married in 1968.

I love to write poetry and read true stories, especially my Bible. I go into the jails and prisons and hold Bible studies with the prisoners in their cells. I work with the missions in downtown Portland, and I hang out with the street kids in the city.

I have been in retail sales for over 30 years, and now I manage a retail store. Peggy has been in the kitchen at a local high school for over 20 years.

We own our home. It has a basketball goal in the driveway and we have two new cars in the garage.

Everything we have, we have accumulated in the past 18 years. I have not had a drink or a drug for over 18 years. I am not religious, but I do have a very strong belief in my higher power, and I choose to call Him God! I attend different churches wherever God takes me, not to seek out a religion, only to share my story of hope.

Here is a short poem I wrote explaining exactly who Don L. Sutton is.

It's me
I have never climbed to a mountain top,
Or crossed the wide open sea.
A trip to the moon I never have made,
I'm just as simple as anyone can be.

I have never witnessed stardom, a trip in its own,
And wealth has never been mine.
I cannot sing, dance, or write songs.
I'm real bland and that is just fine.

Crowds do not gather as I enter a room,
And cheers I never have heard.
Billboards don't reflect the person that I am,
I'm summed up in only one word.

"Common," that's me, and please understand,
I'm as happy as any I know.
I'm real and sincere, myself is my own,
I'm not an act or a fictional show.

I am who I am, who God made me to be,
I'm as strong as a climb to the peak.
Trophies and ribbons are not what I want,
It's my Jesus whom daily I Seek!

It's Me, Don!

E-mail me at BrotherDon@Comcast.net

Dedicated to My Wife and Best Friend, Peggy

This book is dedicated to the only person, without whom it would have been impossible to complete this journey through life, the one person who never gave up on me and was always there when I needed strength and support, the one who desperately strove to keep our family intact and raised our children to be who they are today; we grew up together.

Nearly 40 years of my 55-year journey belong to my wife, Peggy. She endured much pain and hardship to get me where I am today, and I thank her for not ever giving up and always believing in me.

This dedication is a small reward for her outstanding talent and performance. She deserves rubies and diamonds in her crown, but as she is accustomed to, I will have to do!

I love you, Peggy, and please always know that without you, my safe journey would have been impossible. As we continue our journey together, until the end, you will forever be my best friend, and I know from where we have been, we will never return!

With love from your husband and lifelong friend,

Don

Preface

As we travel through life, we are faced with many decisions. Since the beginning of time, decisions have played an important role in survival. Often times, we are required to ask for guidance in order to make correct decisions; other times it is by chance. However you determine the decisions you must make, always remember why you decided as you did. When making decisions, we must also accept the result. Once decisions are made, they are almost always final.

As time passes by, we are often faced with mirrored choices. Choices we may have made, right or wrong, but opportunities later in life to choose again. When these opportunities arise, think before you choose. The results of a decision are factored in at a larger percentage than 50/50. More times than understood, the results are 100 percent, decisions and choices that we are forced to make, often figure in the total outcome. You decide the equation!

Thank you for choosing to take this journey back in time with me. It will be up to you to determine the outcome of your own journey. My outcome has already been decided up to this point in my life, yes, by right and wrong choices I made, while struggling to stay on the straight path. You determine the direction your path will lead you.

My prayer is that you will be led through your own journey differently than I was led through mine. I can only hope that you or whomever you are concerned with will never become as sick as I was. I hope no one is forced to spend their life making the wrong choices that I made; they were nearly fatal! I ask God to keep the same hands over you that He kept over me. Without His protection, we will all be lost. As I learned later in life, He is the right choice. What choice will you make? Remember, it will be right or wrong. It's up to you! One more thing, if you have learned to love others, start learning to love yourself. It is much easier to love others when you are able to forgive yourself and go on. I have learned all about the word EGO, it is Edging God Out! Sit back and share my experience with me. We will share in a short time what has taken me over 50 years to discover. Everything is real. There is no fiction involved, only real live stories. Thank you and enjoy the journey and decide if you will choose freedom or not! My name is in this story numerous times, but always know, this journey is about freedom and letting go of the things which keep us in bondage. Holding on to the past always keeps the future dim. Let go and let God and light will appear on your horizon as it did mine.

Chapter 1
Visions and Dreams

Seven years old, residing in a cheap little apartment in the middle of this great nation, Missouri, the Show Me State, and learning how to retrieve medical devices from the drug store and oh yes, running after cigarettes, accompanied by a note from my mom. A child forced to do something that over time has become as illegal as bank robbery. I recall most of my younger years, my dear mother fighting daily the deadly disease asthma. My brother and I would take turns riding our bike to the drug store and deliver medications back home to our constantly sick mom. That seemed to be the first real chore in life that I didn't mind being responsible for. My brother and I would fight to determine who got to do it. After all, Mom was our hero and we would do whatever we had to do to make her life more comfortable.

My mother and father met after World War II, in Portland, Oregon. Dad was from Omaha, Nebraska, but ended up in Portland with his brother, Clifford. Dad had another brother who played a very important role in my life, and that person was my Uncle Earl. Uncle Earl was the rock in my life. He was the one who owned his home, had the perfect family and always cared for others, especially his own. He was the one everyone ran to for help and advice, the one who always had the answers. As a young child and still, I wonder why the good people seem to die before the bad. I guess they are on loan to us and God has other duties for them in Heaven. Uncle Earl was one of them, God took him home at a young age and I long to see him over there. I know he will be waiting and continue to teach me to be who I need to be. He played a big part in helping me be who I am today!

My dad and his two brothers were deserted by their father when they were very young boys, and their mother was forced to raise their family. This same

11

DON L. SUTTON

lady, later in my journey, would be faced again with the same challenge, only this time there were only two young boys.

I remember one summer night, my brother and I came in from playing outside, and there at the foot of the stairs lay our mom. She was struggling desperately to breathe; the asthma was attacking her again. Dad had just called the ambulance and when he mentioned this, we were terrified.

Dad told my brother and me, "Boys, your mother is very sick. You need to say a prayer for her and ask God to make her well."

So, me being the little young evangelist that I was, I ran to the top of the stairs, darted immediately left and into the little bathroom awaiting my arrival. I ran in, slammed the door, knelt down at my little white porcelain altar and began to recite the Lord's Prayer.

At the close of the prayer, I added a couple lines of my own. "And God, would you please make my mommy well? I don't want her to die!"

I remember weeping as I prayed and I will always see in my mind what happened next. Upon entry, I failed to switch the light on. As I began to weep and beg God for a miracle, that little bathroom lit up like Yankee Stadium. I remember looking up at the little window over the tub and there with an angel standing on each side of Him, was Jesus. Both of His nail-scarred hands were stretched out toward me. I remember the scars; later on in life I would carry my own. There stood the Jesus I had learned so much about in my Sunday school classes at the church we went to on a regular basis. He looked in my eyes, reached down and touched my heart, and then I became so very frightened. I jumped up, slammed myself into the door, then backed up and opened it, ran down the stairs I had just so gallantly climbed, and halfway down I flew through the air into my dad's waiting arms. He caught me, fortunately, and as I began to share with him what had just happened, my dad began to make sense of what had occurred and did what he could to calm me down.

Eventually the ambulance arrived, and by then my mom was sitting up and feeling much better. She didn't have to leave with the ambulance that night and she always attributed her recovery to the visit I welcomed from my good friend, Jesus, in that quaint little tabernacle at the top of the stairs.

To this day I can see Jesus standing and smiling, as He reached His hands out toward me. The picture remained etched in my mind even as my life began

CHOOSE FREEDOM:
THE JOURNEY

to shatter, as I grew older. My dad still recalls that blessed event. He is now 82 years old. I have told that story all my life and will continue until I see Him face to face in Paradise. Then I will thank Him.

Many times in life we are confronted with situations that at the time seem so difficult to find meaning. I searched most of my life for answers to this blessed visit I received from God. I was confused why God would allow such a young person, a little boy, a vision such as this with no voiced explanation. I knew in my heart why the outstretched hands, but I questioned the real meaning.

Eventually 45 years later, I began to see the real reason for my vision. And I say mine because it was something I carried with me through good times and bad. Eventually Jesus would visit me again.

It was January 14, 2002. I was asleep and I began to dream. In the dream I was running down the center of the highway in pursuit of a line of autos. It was as though they were driving to a funeral and I was trying desperately to catch up. The entire string of cars were colored black. I was beginning to tire and become short of breath when we crested the top of the hill. As I reached the top and could see over, I noticed the autos had left me behind. They were nowhere in sight. Just over the hill I came upon a "Y" in the road. Without knowing the direction to follow, I chose the road to the right. As I noticed my energy returning along with my breath, the road stopped. There in front of me stood a big bright building. I noticed the building had no windows, only one large wooden round top door with no locks and no handle. I walked cautiously up to the door and as I placed my finger against it, the door began to open slowly on its own. I peeked inside and off in a distance sat a man all dressed in white silk, covering even His head. He seemed to be sitting on a throne of soft white pillows or a cloud and he was painting a portrait, held on an easel.

As I approached Him slowly, I said to Him, "Excuse me. Could you please help me? I believe I am lost."

He slowly turned His face toward me and it was the same face I had seen in that little window when I was seven.

Jesus looked deep in my soul and responded, "No, you are not lost, you are right where you need to be!"

He then reached over and turned His portrait toward me and it was a painting of Him nailed to the cross. The picture had no color except at the nail holes in His hands and feet, the crown pricks in His forehead and the pierced hole in His side. They were all red. The rest of the portrait was gray.

One other piece of this dream seemed to really stand out in my mind. This was the brush that Jesus held in His hand and was using to paint the picture. It was very large in diameter and very long, red blood dripped off the tip and stained a spot on the floor. What left such an impression in my mind was the fact that He was holding the brush in His left hand, while He was painting, blood was dripping off the end pooling on the floor. This puzzled me until one morning as I was reading my Bible I came across a story in the book of Judges. The story was in chapter 20, verse 16. It is a story about the Israelites fighting the Benjamites. This part of the story explains a bit about perfection, which definitely describes my Jesus. The verse reads, "Among all these soldiers there were seven hundred chosen men who were left handed, each of whom could sling a stone at a hair and not miss." After reading this, I was directed to Judges chapter 3, verse 15, then to 1 Chronicles chapter 12, verses 1-2.

One evening as I was again reading the word, God spoke to me so briefly and subtle and gave me the reason for the brush. His son was perfect with His right and left hand. That was it, a revelation from God that no one had ever shared with me. I did then and still feel so privileged that He would share something unknown to someone as tarnished as me, something no one else had ever been privileged to know.

I have shared this new revelation with a handful of friends and the reason for this journey is beginning to have more substance. Now I will be able to share it with those who choose to take this journey back with me.

Some may ask what significant value this revelation may have, but to me, my prayer is that I would get to know Jesus more. Since I met the master, I have been seeking and searching for Him all the day long and I finally have found Him. He is so real and true, like no one I have ever met! Think of loved ones in your family. Isn't it obvious who is left-handed and who is right-handed? I know it is with me, so now I know just a little bit more about the man named Jesus, the one whom I seek daily now, as my journey continues!

As I began to search for more reasons why Jesus allowed me two personal visits as He did, I began to understand fully. I was led to the book of Joel in

CHOOSE FREEDOM:
THE JOURNEY

the Old Testament, chapter 2, verse 28. I was also led to the Book of Acts in the New Testament, chapter 2, verse 17: "Your young men will see visions; your old men will dream dreams."

Finally, I found the answer I was searching for right in the word, right where all of the answers are. You just have to try and find them in their proper place no matter how long it may take. The answers were right where God said they would be. In Him, He is the answer.

I then awoke and felt as though I was on the most joyful journey I have ever been on, more pleasant than the one I felt led to begin back that morning. I was filled with excitement and joy. This was when I began to seek God as never before! That is also the day He inspired me to write this book, January 14, 2002.

Rest Area

As we begin our journey back through time, back through a time that often still confuses me, as I reminisce, I ask that you travel along with me with an open mind and with an open heart. There are many events we will share together, and as we do, please do not to feel sorry or sad for me. I will share many of my worn-out years openly, as we journey along. I will do so only to allow you to see the pain and heartaches that I, as well as yourself, have experienced in life.

A lot of the pain will be familiar to you and the reason for our adventure back in time is not to dwell on my past, but I want you to realize that terrible things not only happened to you, but many of us share the same tragedies in life, from childhood to adulthood. The purpose of this journey is so you can find the real reason for things that happened to us along the way, the real reason that I discovered, after almost 40 years of living with no hope, so many of the same excuses and reasons for making wrong choices and bad decisions. Remember as we travel along–do not dwell on the past, but keep looking ahead, the future matters now.

Thank you for sharing this lifetime journey with me and please, enjoy the sights along the way. Hopefully the journey will reflect a bit of your past as well and allow you to understand that you are not alone and freedom is knocking at your door.

Chapter 2
Discovering

Seven was a fun age, but each year seemed to get more exciting. Eight was an age of growing, learning about myself and experiencing some of the true values of life. That was a time when there were mommies and daddies, aunts and uncles, grandmas and grandpas, and ponies. It was also a time when there were fewer divorces, real reasons to love and fewer choices to make, evening meals at the table, picnics with friends, family reunions and Sunday dinner at Grandma's house, times when family would gather together to socialize and share recipes with each other, in edible form. I loved the beautiful desserts some would bring and how ugly they would be after everyone took their share. Desserts were my favorite back then and they still are. Food tasted so real when you were young. Probably, because it was!

After lunch, everyone would lay or sit around and complain about how they had overeaten and assure one another they would not do it again. They were forced to indulge because of the appearance or smell of everything on the table. Yeah right, they wouldn't indulge again, not until next Sunday, this was a weekly tradition!

Those were the good old days when the love from one another engulfed us all. Hugs and kisses when everyone arrived and hugs kisses and excuses when everyone departed. A time when everyone seemed to care more for one another and be willing to help each other when needed, unlike today, when everyone is too busy to worry about anyone else or their needs. What happened?

I think I enjoyed it most because it was a time for us to act as if our lives were perfect in every way and that all of our dreams were coming true. A time

CHOOSE FREEDOM:
THE JOURNEY

for all to share what little perfection each one had accomplished in their lives and the new goals they were establishing on their own. Poverty played an important role back then, but we were all so happy, I didn't even notice it. I didn't have video games or skateboards to ride; I had real live little people to play with and they didn't require batteries! On birthdays and Christmas there weren't stacks of presents to open, maybe just one, but that was okay. We realized how hard our parents worked and we didn't expect much. We just wanted to be loved and forgiven for the mistakes we continuously made.

I think that is when I decided when grown-ups were busy with someone else's concerns it left no time for their own. That must be why gossip played an important role in family life back then. Sitting together with our ears stretched together to listen to neighbors having conversation on the telephone party lines; that was a lesson I also learned at an early age. By acquiring this sort of education at such a young age, I was able to apply it to my own life as I grew older.

Another valuable lesson I learned later on in life is that it seems the older you get, the smaller families are. Some may say this is good, but I seem to disagree. Too many people have decided that living life is more important than giving life. As I have grown older, I have determined that family is all you have, and as different circumstances arise, family is all you need. Material gains in life can be taken away but family is yours forever if you choose. If you never let go of the ones you love, they will always remain in your heart and in your mind. The choice is yours, mostly.

Isn't it amazing how you remember the things you aren't supposed to and forget the things you should. I now realize why, when growing up, adults constantly were saying, "Children are to be seen and not heard." I think they were afraid they would be challenged by the truth and possibly learn that they could be wrong!

Well, let's get back to the eight-year-old. Up until that point, I was not one of those little boys who was growing up in a real abusive surrounding. Yes, there were disagreements and family arguments, but I do not recall any major issues up to that point of my life. We were just a family that didn't have much money, but we had a lot of time. So, I guess looking back on the first eight years of my life, things were pretty bland, but good. There was no excuse then for my life to turn out the way that it did. It was a time when I wish I could have stayed in for at least another 20 years, as I knew not what my future would hold. I didn't know the anguish that would lie ahead. Soon the tragedies would begin to unfold without much choice.

Looking back, I am sure there were alcoholics in my family fearing to admit their weaknesses, but none really left an impression on my fast-developing, premature little mind. I do, however, remember sneaking into the cabinets at my grandpa's house and choosing to pry a lid open now and then, and stick my finger in the bottle to get a taste or a smell. I recall how terrible a response I received and was quick to recap the bottles and put them back in their dark little hiding place. That was an exciting adventure. Not to taste or smell but to do it with out being caught.

At the time, I knew it was wrong. Good things were not hidden. Good things were left out in the open like the candy dishes on the table and dirty shoes sitting outside the door. One of the little things that adults fail to realize is that kids don't miss a thing. Children want to learn the reason for things, good or bad, happy or sad. That is what growing up was all about to me. I did, however, make a major decision at that point of my life. I decided to choose soda pop over the alcohol I had been experimenting with from the depths of the cabinets. Soda pop, at that time in my life, had been chosen as my drink of choice. It was much sweeter, didn't smell bad and I did not have to sneak around to enjoy it. What an awesome discovery!

As an eight-year-old growing up, I never experienced my mother or father indulging in any form of alcohol. Stories were later circulated about the times when they were young and experimenting with life as I was, but I guess I chose not to pay a whole lot of attention to what they were doing in their world. I was more involved trying to discover what my own little world was all about. I was more interested in baseball, ice cream, candy, and school. I do remember the stories my dad would share with us kids regarding his term in the Army, during the Second World War. I was so proud of my dad, fighting for my country. I can remember thinking of him each morning at school as we recited the Pledge of Allegiance with my little hand clasped over my heart. Yes, that was another thing I miss about the past. Respect for our country and my dad! Occasionally I would allow my ears to stretch out of shape to bend around corners to hear the adult stories of the war. But looking back, I can truthfully say none of the stories I listened to ever gave me a desire

CHOOSE FREEDOM:
THE JOURNEY

to go get drunk or run out and join the Army. I was too busy deciding what I could do with my own life as I continued to mature.

I wanted to be a preacher! Those were my Sunday school days and the times when I was concerned about my mommy and her health. I remember, as a child, my father was always involved somewhere, somehow in church. I also recall the demands he made on my brother and me to attend church with him. My mom chose not to go with him, for various reasons I choose not to mention, but valid reasons nonetheless.

I recall chasing my brother down the stairs to retrieve the Sunday morning newspaper before the Sunday school bus came to pick us up. Upon returning to our little apartment, the first thing our father would do was rip the comic section up into small pieces while we watched. It was against his religion to allow us or anybody to read comics. We were not allowed to speak any form of slang or our punishment was a mouth washing with a bar of soap. It was amazing how soon I developed a taste for so many different brands of bar soap!

It also was a sin to dance, watch cartoons or look at little girls the wrong way. That was very difficult at such a young age because that was when I started noticing there definitely was a difference between us and I liked what I saw.

I loved to ride the Sunday school bus to church. Each Sunday, it was as though I was going on a mission trip to the Holy Land. I enjoyed standing up in front of the class and nervously trying to quote the verse I had tried so diligently to remember all that week. It was as though I had the attention of the whole world. I felt like a young evangelist. Why I didn't follow my dream, I do not know. Could it have been that I decided against fulfilling my dream? Yes, looking back I do realize that I decided against this first goal in life and as I traveled onward, I made many other choices that were not always right.

Chapter 3
Those Were the Days of Poverty

So now we have arrived at a time in my life when I was ten years old. Little did I realize I had stumbled into a time when the perfection in my life would begin to fade away. This was a fun time as well. I remember swimming, playing baseball, throwing rocks, learning to whistle, mastering the hoola-hoop, losing teeth and all the other fun stuff that came with being a young explorer. And that is exactly what I was at this young age. Tarzan and Jane had come onto the scene and I was Tarzan and the little girl across the alley was Jane. If there was adventure on the horizon, I was the one to call to duty. I was full of mischief and overflowing with energy.

I can remember so clearly the tone of my mom's voice as she shouted from our little kitchen window. Her voice would echo through out the neighborhood that it was time for me to come home. By then, I had learned to distinguish enough to know if the shout was a sounding trumpet call to come home and be loved or a call to retreat and surrender. If it was the latter, I had become accustomed to breaking off a switch from the bushes outside the door and carry it on my way up the stairs, for I knew it was going to be used on me. I would push open the apartment door slowly, knowing that I had been caught again and a whipping was at hand, Mom's hand. I always knew to break off a large switch because if it was too small, she would use it, and then instruct me to go get another one, and she would whip me with both of them. Our landlord always thanked my mom for keeping the bushes trimmed back around the apartment house. He didn't realize the price I was paying to oblige him for such a painstaking chore. It never failed, every time I did something wrong, I got caught. Was someone telling on me or was I just

CHOOSE FREEDOM:
THE JOURNEY

real ignorant at hiding my faults? Now I think it was a training period in my life that I would be accustomed to as I grew older.

I wasn't a bad kid back then; let's just say I was a mischievous little individual, one who always seemed to find a way to not only discover the good things in life, but I was able to find the bad, as well. I made many wrong choices when I was young, such as stealing candy, smoking cigarettes, shooting BB holes in windows, swearing and I was able to make a remarkable discovery about girls, thanks to the Sears and Roebuck catalog at my friend Billy's house. I and a couple of buddies would all meet in the alley. We would set a time and each one of us would go separate ways. We would walk the streets and pick up cigarette butts. We would meet back at our starting point, tear the little bit of tobacco out of the find, roll it in newspapers and smoke them like cigarettes. They sure had a smoother taste than the grape vines that Tarzan and I smoked together!

There was little persuasion involved in most of the discoveries I made; I chose them on my own. And many times I used my power of persuasion to involve my friends as well. It always made the punishment seem worth it when I could share it with someone else. We all seemed to make some bad choices in life, but wasn't that what learning and growing up was all about?

So much time has passed by, but I still remember my mother so well. She has since passed away but I recall her being such an important part of my young life. I was never allowed to tell my brother Dennis, but she always told me I was her favorite. I think she did so because my dad never knew for sure if he was my father or if the milk man could have the honor. Mom, later in life, assured me he was. Instead of blaming her, he always chose to blame me. He and my brother seemed to be closer, but I didn't care. I had a great relationship with my mom. Yes, sneaky little me, the hero of my mom's world. Like Tarzan was to me and Jane was to Tarzan.

I remember lying in bed at night, crawling under the covers and evangelizing in my own little tent revival. Just like the tent healing meetings I would watch on our small black and white television; that was a show we were all allowed to watch! In my little tent, I would invite my mom to come forward for healing and Jesus would heal her every time. Yet, in reality, Mom did not want anything to do with church or religion. She always told me she believed in God and the day before she died, I had the privilege to pray with her. Not going to church was a choice she made and one I never truly understood, except that we all make different choices.

I recall my father inviting her but she would always refuse. He wouldn't take her dancing or out to eat, so she didn't feel it was necessary to go with him to church. She did, however, encourage my brother and me to go. I think she thought it could do us good and it did!

I also recall my mom not having very many personal belongings. Prescription drugs were what made her the happiest. Before she passed away, she was so addicted to prescription drugs, she just continued to get sicker and sicker. Because of her addiction to pain killers, she missed out on the honor of being a grandmother. Because of her choice to live the way she did, she died at 52 years of age. She missed out on a lot of life, but she always told me she could never get over leaving my dad and us boys. There is one choice that my mom made that changed the lives of our entire family. It seemed like everything Mom had was just sufficient enough to get her by, especially if it came in a pill form. I remember feeling sad for her, as I would be invited into my friend's homes and see what their mommies were blessed with. But hey, she had me, what more could a lady in her twenties have to live for?

Chapter 4
Disaster Strikes

I remember one hot summer day; Mom spent her last five dollars at the second-hand store. She purchased an old red worn-out bicycle for my brother and me. She had really become our hero at that point of our young lives. That was a time when experience did not play into our world much. Little did we know then, that this new bicycle would play a very important role in the most disappointing chapter of our life, a beginning to an end, like a flat tire!

I remember day after day, riding that old worn-out bike, me on the handlebars and Dennis at the controls. We would ride to the baseball field in the morning, play ball till noon, ride back home for lunch, then back to the swimming pool until four in the afternoon and back home to play in the alley till dark. Swimming sometimes was free as our best friend's sister was a lifeguard. Baseball was sponsored by some local organization and the alley that ran behind our house was the meeting place for the neighborhood gang. We were a different kind of gang back then, kind of like the Little Rascals. The only trouble we caused would only affect ourselves. We were not into damaging property too much or anything that did not belong to one of us, except maybe pumpkins. We all knew we would get disciplined and back then it hurt! We were mostly into having fun and bonding with one another, real pals. What an ideal lifestyle. What could be better? Well, it wasn't long before our world began to tarnish.

One morning, our mom rewarded Dennis and me for being two outstanding boys that week. I wasn't concerned about her making a false judgment that morning; I was more concerned about the reward. I remember

Mom handing us both a crisp new one dollar bill. She instructed us to not come home after baseball. The money was for lunch at the pool and she hoped we would enjoy ourselves together, spending the entire day doing what we did best, having fun. We were rich! What in this big wide world had we done to warrant such a reward? This was the most money we had ever received at one time. We were both millionaires. (I must mention, I have not since had that feeling of wealth, at least not with money.)

I remember as Mom sat us both down and began telling us how much she loved us and how much she appreciated all we had ever done for her. She explained that if anything ever happened to her, she would always love us. We really didn't want to hear what she was telling us, but we allowed her to have her victory speech; after all she had just spent two bucks for her time in the spotlight. We felt obligated to listen, but all we wanted to do was get on that old bike and ride like the wind. She finally told us goodbye, kissed us and we left her and our little sister Debbie in our tracks.

I think we got that old used bicycle up to record speeds that day. We were both on top of the world (actually I was on top of the handle bars). The world that had been so limited had just allowed us more than we felt we deserved. We were so happy that morning. I recall Dennis and I playing the best baseball of our careers that day. I remember getting up enough courage that day to jump off the high dive. I also remember what I spent my entire fortune on and what I had to eat at the pool—one hot dog with mustard and relish, package of potato chips, Milky Way candy bar, chocolate fudge cycle and an ice cold bottle of soda pop, all that for a buck, what a deal. I do not recall any sadness after spending the whole dollar; I just remember having to wait an hour before I could get into the water.

The dollar excited us so much because those were the days of poverty. There were many days when we would only eat one meal a day and that was usually in the evening and it came in a can. I remember many days going to school without a lunch or money to buy lunch and lunch at school was only 25 cents. I would stay in my class, wait for everyone to leave and I would take out my Big Chief tablet and begin to fix my own lunch. I would draw pictures of meats, cheese, slices of bread, pickles and tear up strips of paper to serve as lettuce. I would draw round imperfect circles and pretend they were potato chips. I would then cut out the pictures with my little dull scissors

CHOOSE FREEDOM:
THE JOURNEY

and begin to make me a delicious sandwich. I would substitute mayonnaise with school paste, and when finished, I would make certain no one was watching, I would close my eyes and begin to enjoy my lunch. I would imagine that it was real and I would pretend to savor every bite. If I had extra paper I would cut out cookies and draw chocolate chips on them and cut them out and they would satisfy my sweet tooth. And I'd top my feast off at the drinking fountain in the hall. I can still hear the hum of my belly as I sat in class and tried to concentrate on why I was even there.

After school, I would walk home and on the way I would go into the little grocery store, lean down into the ice cream cooler and steal bites from ice cream bars, and if no one followed me down the aisle, I would take bites out of cupcake packages, biting through the wrapper and swallowing it too. I was hungry. Thinking back, I wonder if it was possible then or even now, for me to blame my alcohol and drug addiction on poverty or hunger. No, I think that excuse would be lame. I am still poor!

Well, Dennis and I climbed back on our little second-hand bike and flew home to explain to our mom what a wonderful day we had, thanks to our hero; we had just had the best day of our lives.

As we were peddling down the street approaching our corner of the world, there was our grandmother walking toward us. She had just gotten off the bus and was treading toward our apartment house for a visit. What a delightful ending to such a fun and special day. We hurried to meet her. I jumped off the handlebars, ran over and grabbed one of her bags, then grabbed her free hand and began to share all the terrific surprises that unfolded that day. We began to share in perfect harmony the events that had taken place on that special fun-filled day. We wanted the whole world to know what a great mom we had and that she could outdo anyone. It was the best day of our lives, we thought.

We reached the apartment and up the stairs we ran, 21 to be exact. I always was one to count them, in a hurry or not.

Dennis and I threw open the door and in harmony one last time, we both shouted, "MOM!"

All we got in return was an echo, ours. No sounds, no Mom, no sister, only a scribbled-out note leaning up against the telephone. I can still see that note. Grandma picked up the note and began to read it to herself. We both asked

25

why she was crying and all she could say was that she would let our dad explain it to us when he got home from work.

Wow, a day filled with rewards and excitement had just developed into a day of total confusion, a day that would etch itself into my mind and into the hearts of our entire family, never to be forgotten.

Later that evening, Dad shared the letter with us and tried not to directly indicate that our hero had just stolen away our baby sister and left us deserted and lost. She had tricked us! My mom, the one whom God had healed under my cover in my private tent meetings, Mom, the one whom I had prayed for and talked to my Jesus about, the one, who rewarded us earlier that day, had now taken our trophies back. A verdict had been reversed, what could have gone wrong?

The question is, could this be the reason for the life I chose to live? Could this be the excuse I have been searching for? Is this the reason I chose to become an alcoholic and a drug addict? My answer continues to be no. Alcohol or drugs never entered my mind that dreadful day. All I could think about that day was the loss of two of my closest friends—a mother who tried to teach me right from wrong and always made me believe that her life was complete with me and a sister with whom I enjoyed playing more than any other toy I had. Both of them were gone from my life and I was so sad.

Yes, I did finally find it in my heart to forgive her for the scar she had inflicted on me, but I still struggle with the fact that it happened. Mom made a terrible choice that day and as I have learned much about decision making, if she had another opportunity to make the same choice, the result would obviously be the same. I do not feel angry at her because God has taught me so much, but I still can't understand how parents can give away something so precious that God has given them—life. All through my life I wondered if she was as sad that day as I was. I will never know, but I must admit that because of her mistake, I had decided if I grew up and had children, I would never leave them, but I did, night after night.

Chapter 5
Off Limits

Life continued on from that day. Things began to fall back in place as Grandma decided to move in with us. Grandma tried so desperately to be our new mom, but she was still our grandma. It was harder on her than it was on us boys and a whole lot harder than when she was young and deserted by her husband. She did an awesome job taking care of and raising my dad and his two brothers, but she was tired and worn out, yet she gave it all she had. We continued at our high rate of speed but Grandma was getting sick. She already had raised a family on her own. Now, to have it to do it again was difficult, but she maintained. I admire her so much still for her love and courage. She added so much strength back to our weakened world.

Included in the package with Grandma came an older man named Jack. He was a friend of Grandma's and he wanted to come into our world and bring with him the title of Grandpa. We had never really had a grandpa in our life. Why not give it a try? Dennis was a little more hesitant than I was, but he wasn't as desperate as me. Dad and Dennis were closer, so I decided to give Jack a try.

Jack called me Skipper and anything I wanted to do, he would give me a chance to try. He drove an old red Studebaker pickup and to this day, whenever I see a truck like his, I cringe. We would drive down the roads hunting for rabbits on the weekends and on Friday nights Grandma, Jack and I would take in a wrestling match and then hunt worms afterwards for our fishing trip the following morning. Jack and I fished together. He taught me how to ice skate; he bought me baseballs and bats, fishing poles, ice cream and he even allowed me to drive his old boat occasionally. He and I found

27

an old wooden ironing board at the local dump spot and he took it and made a surf board for me and pulled me behind his old fishing boat. Finally, I had found a replacement for the loss that had recently occurred. Here was someone I could trust and enjoy the fun things in life, or so I thought.

About a year after Jack came into my life, when I was eleven years old, I was allowed to spend the summers with Grandma and Jack. They lived on a lake and we would have summer days filled with fun and excitement. My life seemed to be back in full swing again when suddenly it happened, another tragedy. This is how it started.

Living on the lake where we did, we had no running water. Jack and I would take the boat to the backside of the lake and take a bath every night. We would both get naked and try to get as clean as we could in the muddy water. One evening, he decided to teach me how to take a bath like a man. It confused me because I thought I was still a little kid. He began to touch me in places I had been taught were off limits to everyone but me. I was scared to death but I had instilled so much trust in this man, I thought what he was doing was for my own good.

He continued to reach deeper and deeper into this act every time we were alone. He began to force me to touch him in places where I should not have been allowed, but I didn't want to lose the only friend I had. So many times when I was around other family members I just wanted to shout out what was going on between me and this perverted old man but Jack always instructed me to keep quiet because no one would believe me. He told me that I had been caught in so many little lies trying to get out of trouble that he convinced me I would be the guilty one and our friendship would be over and all the free stuff would disappear.

I had to make one of the most difficult decisions of my life, another choice, and one that no one should be required to make, especially not an eleven-year-old child. He was sick but I was too young to realize it.

So, I made the wrong choice that day. I kept quiet! I went along with the filthy scheme Jack had added to my life and I lived in fear every day of my young life. I never knew from one day to the next what was going to happen to me, what Jack was going to force me to do to him or what he was going to try with me. I was scarred again, only this time I couldn't talk to anyone about it!

CHOOSE FREEDOM:
THE JOURNEY

Jack would take me up to the local store and as I sat and ate my ice cream cup and drank my soda pop, he would sit and visit with a few other grandpas and I remember them honoring him for taking me under his wing and doing what he did for me. So many times, I wanted to interrupt and tell them the truth, but Jack had already convinced me no one would listen. So, I sat and enjoyed my treat as slowly as I could. I knew what was next and it was not something to look forward to. This happened every day, not just once in awhile! I knew that around every corner of my path there would be disaster waiting. One of the only things about my life I really can't recall is the amount of times I just wished I would die!

Looking back on that terrible sickening situation, I still do not remember wanting to run out and get drunk over what was happening to me. Alcohol, marijuana or cocaine never entered my mind then, so how would I be able to choose to use it as an excuse at a later time in life? My drink of choice was still soda pop and I had no desire to switch to alcohol. I did, however stay sane. I need not try to understand how, but I need to accept the facts.

The sexual abuse continued until I was 14. Three years of total lost time, a time when having fun had no real meaning any longer. Fear had crept into my life and everywhere I turned it awaited. This time in my life would have to be considered the worst. How could someone you trusted in so much hurt you so terribly?

Many of you have been faced with similar situations and I share your sadness. I have, however, a difficult time understanding why individuals elect to treat someone like Jack treated me, but I also have a difficult time understanding why people use these hurts for excuses to ruin their life even more. Personally, I never used the perversion for an excuse for how or why I lived my life. I would not allow this perverted individual the satisfaction of ruining the rest of my life, as he did his.

If I dig deep, I can still recall the fear and disappointment that went along with this terrible act, but I choose not to dwell on it. I have since forgiven the man for his sinful act against me and my one wish is that Jack found God before he died and I pray he made it to heaven.

Chapter 6
The Fairy Tale Began

Eventually my father met a woman in the church we were attending and they were married. She was to be our new mom. She was a good lady but she and my dad were so caught up in religion, I had a difficult time adjusting.

My brother and I were now cast into the scenes from the movie, *Cinderella*. We both were now dreaded stepchildren. We moved to our new mom's territory, out of the city and into the country. We lived near her family and we were required to adapt to their lifestyle. The days of walking to school, playing baseball in the alley and swimming at the pool were now remnants of the past. Now it was hitting rocks on the gravel road, swimming in the muddy pond and riding the cold school bus down the rough, dusty roads.

We adapted fairly easy to the fun stuff but the chores were more difficult to understand–grinding corn, feeding the chickens and milking the cow were not necessarily on the to-do list of two city boys. However, those were the days when you had no choice but to respect and obey your elders. You did what you were told and you did not have a choice in the matter. When you were instructed to do something your mind had already been made up for you, just like it should be today. We didn't have metal detectors in our schools back then. We took manners and lambs to school, not guns and knives.

The switches were bigger in the country and there were more of them. Dennis and I adapted quite well to our new environment, but it wasn't the world we were accustomed to. I was, however, very happy I had escaped the sexual abuse by Jack and I was not feeling any loss when he departed

CHOOSE FREEDOM:
THE JOURNEY

from my world. I remember the day he died, mixed emotions. I wasn't going to miss him; I just hoped he was ready to meet God, his choice, not mine.

Moving into the country also added some benefits. Dennis and I shared a room together on the bottom floor. No more running up and down those 21 stairs. He and I did, however have arguments over who was going to sleep by the window. I always lost, of course. The window selection was all right in the summer but in the winter I would wake up in the night and shake the snow from my covers. It was a quaint little place with no water or indoor plumbing. We didn't enjoy walking out to the barn to relieve ourselves but you did what you had to do. I remember the excitement throughout the house when Dad surprised us with our new outdoor toilet. It even had a light in it. We had moved up with the neighbors. We survived with what we had. Besides we were country folk now and that was the way Dad chose for us to live.

Dad did his best to provide for the church and us. We, in turn, did what we could to adjust and pitch in to help make ends meet. We worked every day except Sunday. We would work this day as well if the oxen were in the ditch and it seemed to be mostly every Sunday. Our father was involved heavily in church most of his life, and like it or not, we went along. Those continued to be the days when, because of religion, we were not allowed to go to parties at school, watch the Beatles on *Ed Sullivan*, or speak any type of slang. When bad thoughts crept into our minds, we got spanked. Sometimes rules were good, but mostly they were out of line. Being told you would spend eternity in a pit of fire for reading *Tom and Jerry* was a little too tough for me to swallow. If this was a God my father expected me to bow down to, he was wrong. Perfection was not one of my better traits.

I recall one of my father's mini-sermons he delivered to me one day while I was still young and adhering to rules. He told me I needed to make a decision some time in my life. That decision was to choose this God of his or Satan. Which one was I going to decide to live for? He instructed me that whichever I decided to follow, give it my all. This seemed to be a fairly easy decision to make, especially after the experiences I had, growing up in a so-called church home. I witnessed divorce, adultery, lust, abuse, desertion and now I was required to make a decision of this magnitude. I observed what went on in the church that we were required to attend and it wasn't good or

God. It was pure religion with a capital R for Rehearsed. This was an easy decision for me to make. "Pass me the bottle!" After all, I seemed to remember the church people in the Bible, nailing my best friend to the cross.

I decided at a very young age that I didn't want anything to do with a God that was so demanding. I often wondered why God would give me life, watch over me and then take it away, only to destroy me. I later learned to know a different God, one who would love and protect me as I traveled this journey. The one who had stretched His nail-scarred hands toward me that day at that little porcelain altar. He was the one I would eventually choose to serve and obey. As we get farther along in our journey, I will explain how and where I met this God I choose to love.

I began an escape at that point in my life. Things weren't going the way they seemed they should, in the storybooks I had read. Why was reality so different than made-up situations? The make-believe seemed so satisfying and sometimes so real. I was at a crossroads in my life where it was time to make up my own fairy tales. I didn't know how, but I was determined to figure it out.

My life thus far had been filled with hurt and pain and I was beginning to grow tired. This should never be forced on a child, but it had been, and I was ready to deal with whatever hand was dealt me. I was ready to figure things out on my own. It was time to learn how to be sneaky and manipulative, and it was time to learn how to blend in with others out of religion. Seemed as though the ones I decided to blend in with didn't have the perfect life, either. There were others out there who had it just as bad as I did. It was easy bonding with them because we could sit around and drink our blues away, together. We could pour our sorrows out of our souls and refill them with real poison.

Yes, it was time to start making some of my own choices in life. Besides, I was 14 years old and I knew everything. Living in the country, it seemed easier to sneak around and do what I wanted to do. There was more room and fewer people than in the city. I decided it was time to experiment with life's more challenging attractions. I had heard stories from the older boys of how, when you got drunk, your problems would all leave. I heard this was a way to escape from the real and pour your guts out to the beer demon.

Well, they were wrong. I would pour my guts out but it was usually on the

CHOOSE FREEDOM:
THE JOURNEY

ground. I would hang out with boys around the dusty neighborhood and they would steal alcohol from their parents' cabinets. I didn't care how they got it just as long as they did and they were willing to share it with me. We would covey up at the end of the road and begin our escapes, together. I didn't like the taste of beer at first, but when you continued to get caught pouring this valuable liquid onto the ground, you eventually were required to adapt to the taste. I did!

I was becoming an alcoholic without actually realizing it. The more I chose to drink, the easier it became. The sips seemed to be tasting better as I continued to force them on myself. Looking back on this new discovery, I can truthfully say I never had anyone push me down and pour anything down my throat. I chose to do it on my own. A few beers a week; what harm could that be? As long as I didn't overdo it, I would be all right. Little did I know that I would be spending the next several years proving that theory wrong.

By the age of 16, I had acquired a taste for beer. During high school our dad would not allow us boys to have a key to our house. The reason for no key was so when we returned home from dates or outings, we would be required to wake him so he could smell our breath and determine if we had been smoking or drinking. Yes, there were times when the Dentine gum and the mouth wash failed to be our only salvation, and when that happened we were transferred to lock-down for a determined amount of time. Often times, I did discover how to pass these terrifying tests but I seemed to fail them more and more.

I chose to discover ways to manipulate the system and these discoveries could and would play a major role later on in our journey on down the road. The tests that I was required to take every time I left the property helped me to become a liar and a con artist. I was bound and determined to figure out a way to get over on my dad, and I did! He actually was teaching me more than he was prohibiting me from doing. I wish now that he would have been more open and helped me through what I was doing instead of condemning me for everything I did. It was so difficult to live up to his standards, so why even try?

33

Chapter 7
Paralysis, The Miracle

I met a sweet young girl named Peggy in school and we decided right away we were meant for each other. We fell in love and dated all through high school. She was a cheerleader and I was a wannabe football star. She was Miss Popular and I was Mister Popular. The main difference between us was she was born and raised in a healthy family environment and my family experience was not so spicy. Peggy's mom and dad didn't agree with what my family life had been and they did their very best to change my lifestyle. They wanted me to be a friend of the family, but not a member of theirs, but this little country girl and I were bound and determined to be one and eventually we did just that and we still are one!

Do you ever remember things happening in your life and you not being able to totally understand why it happened? I want to share a night during our high school days that will forever be etched in my mind. Later in life the true meaning would be uncovered but right then it was a night of confusion. I had made so many wrong choices up to this point in my life and I honestly believe God was teaching me that I was not indestructible. I was still in His hands as He had showed me before.

It was our senior year. Peggy and I had made plans to double date with her best friend and a young boy she had just met. I was told he had a Dodge Charger and he liked to drink. Wow! A fun-filled evening ahead for the preacher's kid. I was thrilled!

I remember the kick-off that night at the football game. I kicked the ball and the big boy on the opposing team received it. The opponent came pounding down the field right into my waiting arms. I had stopped the ball

34

CHOOSE FREEDOM:
THE JOURNEY

carrier but nearly killed myself doing it. The next thing I remember was walking over to the side of the field and passing out again. The next time I came to was in the emergency room at the hospital. I had a broken neck. I was paralyzed on my entire right side. I would never be able to walk again; I would be a paraplegic the rest of my life. My football career was over and so was a life filled with hope and adventure. This was a difficult time in my life. All the things I had decided to do were just a dream. Hope was only a four-letter word.

My dad and brothers left the hospital late the night and as they were traveling the highway home, the Charger that I didn't get to drink or ride in that night, pulled out in front of them. As they rounded the next corner, there the Charger sat in dust and smoke, wrapped around a light pole. Coincidentally it was the infamous, "Dead man's curve." My dad hurried over to the young boy and the young man died in my father's arms. He was, however able to say a prayer before he breathed his last breath. I have often wondered if I would have been given the same opportunity as he was given had I been in the car with him as planned. I should have been there but I lay paralyzed in the hospital, miles away from where I might have been dead.

God did, however, decide to perform yet another miracle in my life during that chain of events. I had family praying for me and God decided to heal me of my injury. I recall the nurses preparing to transfer me to a medical university for a surgery that would leave me unable to care for myself the remainder of my life. The doctor had already had a conference with my family and told them I would be unable to care for myself the rest of my life.

As I was waiting arrival of my transportation, my dad asked the doctor to please check me for movement one last time. He agreed and as he poked me one more time with his little sharp instrument, I flinched. He began to test my entire right side and all the feeling was back.

The doctor sat in the chair next to my bed and with tears in his old worn-out eyes, he admitted this was his first miracle he had ever witnessed. The surgery was cancelled and I left the hospital and went home two days later.

Totally healed and ready to pick up where I had left off, I convinced my coach to allow me to play the last football game of the year and I remember making the last tackle of the game. What a comeback! You would think that after such a miraculous event in my life it would force me to change—no, not me. I was still hurting from the scars that had been applied to me in my younger years and I had made up my mind to continue the endless road I was traveling on, and I did.

Peggy and I began to do things we shouldn't have at a very young age, but after all, Jack had trained me and taught me things I shouldn't have known. He had taught me everything we needed to know. I chose to use his schooling on a tender young country girl who had innocence we chose to destroy. We were engaged right out of high school and after an engagement deadline of one year, we were still not allowed to marry. Peggy's mom and dad could see right through me, but Peggy was blinded by love. We decided we were going to get married one way or the other and we didn't care who liked it. I was beginning to use the manipulation training that I had received back when I was a little boy.

We had been married seven months when we were blessed with a little boy we named Robby. Wow, I was a king. I had made all the right choices and no one could stop me now. I was so proud of my new son; I couldn't wait to leave the hospital and go tell the world of my new treasure. I wanted to go celebrate and receive my rewards in liquid form. I was going out to get drunk and celebrate and that is exactly what I did. I stayed out all night and drove from bar to bar handing out cigars and being rewarded with drink after drink. I got so drunk that night that I literally forgot what I was celebrating. Looking back, I wasn't really celebrating anything, I was just using this event in my life to do what I enjoyed doing–getting drunk. I do believe that time in my life was the real beginning of my life of alcoholism.

Chapter 8
As I Grew Older

I was now 19 years old. Hard to imagine in just 19 years anyone would have experienced the things in life that I had. I was married, a father and continuing a life of total disaster. How could I even think of blaming this situation for all my wrong choices? There was no one to blame but myself. I had acquired all the excuses I needed, but I couldn't choose to pass the blame on to someone else or even on some event that had occurred in my past. It was I who had decided to make the choices, not anyone else. It was too late to wonder if the decisions I had made were good ones or not. Suddenly, they were in living form–children.

Today, I do not regret having my son, Robby. He has grown to be my prince and I thank God for him daily. I wasn't ready for a child, but I had one. It was time to move on and do my best to raise him the way I should.

I remember my little country girl, Peggy. She was such a good mother and wife. I was so undeserving of her and everything she did for me. Sometimes I relied on her, I think, to be the mother that I never had. She was the first real person in my life, since my mom had chosen to desert me when I was a child. I remember coming home drunk and snuggling up next to her and pretending she was the only one in the world. The problem was, she loved me so much that she played into my hand and allowed me to use my mom as an excuse to destroy our relationship. But by the grace of God I still have her.

I also was blessed with a daughter, Becky, who was and still is the light of my world. She kept me on my toes and grew up to be just like me. Not in all ways, but in some. She was a discoverer and a risk-taker as well. Robby

37

DON L. SUTTON

was mommy's boy and Becky was daddy's girl. This was a perfect scenario for someone who thought he had all the right answers in life.

With two little kids at home, Peggy was unable to escort me as I went out into the world in search of adventure. She was so shy and quiet. Peggy would stay home and comfort and raise our children while I searched the world for answers. I would hurry home from work, clean up and create some kind of excuse to leave for the evening. Many times I would not return for days. I thank God for a wife willing to sacrifice herself for the well-being of her children and me, a wife who spoke wedding vows to me and meant every word she said. She is still like that today and I have decided the world needs more Peggys!

Rest Area

As we started this journey, I requested you not feel sad or sorry for any of the events that took place in my life. Please recall, I am only sharing these events to explain one thing. When you discover the real reason why I made the decisions that I did, at the end of this journey, you can discover the same hope that I found. Please understand I am not proud of the lifestyle I chose to live, but if any one thing sounds familiar to you, understand that you need not continue on the endless road you are traveling. As we continue together, I will be sharing many disturbing but true events that took place in my life. They are true stories and ones I try desperately to erase from the journal in my mind. I am ashamed but pleased God allowed me His grace to make it through. Can you see all the excuses building up and reason for me to put the blame on these wrong acts against me? I was building an account of excuses that I could borrow from any time I needed. If you can relate to any of my situations, don't stop reading. You are getting closer to the reason we choose to do what we do. It is so simple.

Chapter 9
Beginning to Learn

Upon my returns from my lost weekends, I always had an excuse for what I had done and a promise to quit living the way I was; sound familiar? That was a day in time when there were states that allowed 18-year-old children to buy beer and drink it. I acquainted myself with these establishments until I was 21 years old. By then, thanks to the decisions I had rendered upon myself, I had substituted my drink of choice. I switched from soda pop to beer. I had tested this new drug enough to know that I could adapt to the taste, the smell and everything else that went along with my new drink. I was settling into the lifestyle of an alcoholic without truly realizing my fate.

I had plenty of excuses why my life had gone where it had, but I was also at a junction of not caring. I was beginning to be someone I never realized could exist—a drug addict. My drug of choice then was beer, harmless, socially acceptable, excusable, sickening beer. I was hooked on the number-one drug in the world, but how? I did not want to be what I was becoming, but it seemed at the time, I had no choice. It was too late to turn back now. Final decisions had been made and I was convinced I was what I was, a drunk, just what society labeled me!

Who or what could I blame it on? I surely could blame it on someone or something. At least that was what I had been told by all the experts. I was told about other people who had become alcoholics due to different reasons. Some described it as a disease, some elected to believe it was hereditary and others explained their own theory of it being in my genes. So here was a list of excuses I could choose from to suit my own character and I wouldn't have to blame it on myself.

39

DON L. SUTTON

Okay, it was settled; I could point the finger at Jack. He was the cause for my addiction, the reason why I had acquired a taste after forcing it in my mouth so many times. But what did that situation have to do with alcohol? Jack didn't drink at all and while Jack was administering his constant acts of perversion on me, never did I feel like running out and getting drunk. So much for that reason.

Okay, Mom. No she didn't drink, either. All she ever did was take prescription drugs every day of her life and the day I discovered she had deserted and left me behind, running out and getting stoned never entered my mind. Mom took pain medication every day, doctor's orders, so that was all right.

The church and God. He was big enough to take the blame, but should I place it on Him? I knew He was watching over me so I decided not to lay it on Him. I didn't want to upset God. It seemed as though He was the only one who hadn't harmed me during my life of hurting and torment. He was always there to talk to and he never deserted me, I realized that.

So finally I decided, I have no one else to blame but myself. I made the choices all my life, right or wrong. What and who gave me the authority to place the blame on someone else or something that occurred years ago? That would definitely be a lie and an outright excuse! I recall people asking me if I knew I had a problem and I would respond with this remark, "No, I drink, get drunk, no problem." It was a wise remark but I meant it.

I understood what I was doing and how I was living was not normal, but I enjoyed the escape from reality and I invited all the attention I was receiving. I was becoming a star in the eyes of everyone who knew me. I couldn't see the clouds, between me and the ones who were judging me. I was becoming blind to the effects of my wrong decisions. Seemed like when I was young, the only attention I received was when I did something wrong. Very seldom was I acknowledged when I did something right. So the more I did wrong the more attention I received. It helped me put my priorities in order, right or wrong.

Chapter 10
Becoming of Age

Finally, I made it to the ripe old age of 21. Now I would be able to find my drug whenever I needed it, even in the grocery stores.

I remember the party I had for myself that day over 30 years ago. I had to do all the planning and invite all my guests because it wasn't such a joyous event to the rest of my family. I invited over 50 of my so-called friends and later was told over 100 had attended my celebration. I did not know who was there because I had a tendency to pass out before the party started, before the guests ever arrived. Peggy would just sit in the corner and harbor Robby and Becky while these fellow drunks would attempt to steal and destroy everything we owned, which wasn't much. She would complain, but I failed to listen. I can still see the fear in her and the children's eyes as everyone attempted to have fun, while I lay on the side and wallowed in my vomit. Peggy was always there to comfort me during my hangovers, especially while I was promising her this was the last time. I probably committed to her to stop drinking every other day for over 20 years.

Shortly after my twenty-first birthday, my drink of choice had been changed again. The beer that I had hated so long ago became a friend to me. I became unable to escape from reality on such a weak drug, so I replaced it with whiskey. A real man's drink–after all, I had been taught to take a bath like a man, now it was time to be trained to drink alcohol like one. What an accomplishment from someone who didn't even like the taste. I soon would find out it worked the same way with other drugs, and I chose to allow it to happen.

It wasn't too long before I could climb into my 3,000-pound missile and drive anywhere as good as anyone. I was so fortunate I never wrecked and destroyed anyone's family, but I guess the God whom I had chosen not to blame for my bad decisions still had His hands over my life. I was the best driver on the road, even though I couldn't see it. I had hundreds of blackouts while driving and while I was intoxicated the roads seemed wider and the car seemed longer. I remember getting up the next morning to see if my car was outside. I would sit and try to figure out how and when I got home and what route I had taken.

Peggy and I still reminisce about all the times I would convince policemen to take me home instead of to jail. Those were the days when getting caught driving drunk required a slap on the hand. That was a time when policemen didn't view drunk driving the same way they do today.

I would be stopped by the police on my way home and drunk. I was such a con artist and manipulator; I would always be able to talk my way out of a ticket. I had worked the system for so long that I was a real pro. I could force myself to cry and dream up stories that even I would believe by the time I was done. I can still see the officers walking up to my door, with me in the back seat of the police car, and watch them wake my Peggy up, only to give her my keys and threaten her to not let me go back after my car. They didn't realize it, but I wouldn't have been able to remember where my car was. One time it took me two days to find it and I can still remember lies that I had to make up and often times, still today, I get caught talking about those lies. I still catch myself believing some of the stories that I had made up. To have to watch for lies that are 30 years old–one can only imagine how real I made them sound.

Later on in life I recall telling myself, I wished that just one time the police would have taken me to jail instead of home. I now realize that I spent most of my life on the wrong side of the bars, sitting on a stool!

Chapter 11
Discovering New Drugs

Marijuana

Then one day, while I was in my early twenties, the unexpected began to happen. I was introduced to a new drug in a form other than liquid. I was introduced to marijuana, something I knew existed but only bad people indulged in this form of escape, a real drug. I remember being coaxed into smoking it for the first time. *I will try this, but I will never do real drugs,* I had decided, the drugs I had read about out in California. I remember thinking about all the troubled kids who must exist out on the West Coast. I felt safe in my little innocent part of the world. Yeah right!

Little did I know at the time that I had already become addicted to the mother of all drugs, the king of beers, the light of the world, the sultan of vomit, plain old alcohol? Could this be true?

I was looked down upon by so many family members and friends for something they were doing as well. I recall seeing them at the same clubs on the weekends and then hearing about them attending church the following morning. One thing I remember my dad saying about me was that at least I wasn't one of those hypocrites from church. I let everyone know what I was doing and very seldom did I try to hide it. Most of those church people were getting their drugs from me, but I was the bad one! Did they not understand the true reason for my life of disaster–alcohol! I remember thinking finally something had turned up in my life that could not alter my mind but a definite way to get rich. The only choice I would have to make was either to enjoy it myself or distribute it to others and reap the benefits. Or possibly, I could do both. I had already decided I could do with or without it, so what was the issue.

43

Well, the foolproof plan failed. The more I purchased, the more friends I accumulated and the farther in debt I became. I discovered a way to find this drug whenever I wanted it. I began purchasing in small amounts and was eventually led to a source where I would purchase 80-pound bales at a time, usually four of them. It was an endless cycle with absolutely no gain. I couldn't believe my business venture was turning sour. I had spent so much of my paychecks on the venture and sacrificed so much of my time that I had saved for my children. What could an expert as smart me be doing wrong? Then one day my luck changed again.

Speed

Right when I felt all hope for success had disappeared, my friend from high school returned from Vietnam. He wasn't over there trying to win the war for our country; he was over there experimenting with new drugs. He told me that was his plan before he got drafted. He came home with a drug that would put us on easy street, a drug that we could sell and make huge profits with, a drug that even members of my family seemed to enjoy–speed. I began to purchase these little demons one million at a time.

There were all kinds of excuses for people to consume this new drug. Weight loss, vacations, work schedules and even stress. Finally a way to reap huge rewards. Some of my best customers were family members who were on diets. It was okay in the eyes of everyone if you were taking this drug to lose weight, but it was bad if you were using it to just get high.

Well, you know where I was at with it, I was a junkie! I designed a new foolproof plan. All I needed to do was set up shop in the park, give away a few free samples and refrain from taking too many myself. I would only need to take one or two a day and this would allow me to keep the shop open way into the night. *Perfect plan*, I thought. It wasn't long until I was taking five to ten of these innocent little bombs an hour and eventually found myself taking as many as 50 a day. I remember the day I ended up in the emergency room from an overdose and the doctor telling me I was lucky that I did not die. I wasn't lucky, I was just good! All the benefits I had worked into my plan were slowly slipping away. I couldn't believe a mastermind as myself failed again.

CHOOSE FREEDOM:
THE JOURNEY

LSD/Acid

As my failure was becoming so evident, another form of success entered into my domain. I remember the fear that came over me as I was introduced to acid (LSD). This was one of the drugs I had read about that was destroying so many young people in other parts of the country. How could something this powerful ever have found its way back onto my little gravel road? Was it luck or fate? I would soon learn that it was fate. I decided right away that there had come a time when I decided that if I was ever going to get rich dealing drugs, I had to learn to make myself refrain from getting too acquainted with this little demon. I was purchasing them a few thousand at a time. It was worth a try.

I was 23 years old by then and I had become a real genius. I had discovered ways to manipulate everyone around me and I had been given a new title, "The best con artist in town." Finally, I was a star in my own eyes. I just wasn't twinkling. I was a number-one con artist not realizing everyone else knew it as well. I could get one over on anyone; I was ready to conquer the world. Not realizing the world had conquered me, the world of drugs, that is.

One day as I was finally realizing a profit from my new business venture, I decided to find out what was so demanding and entertaining about this new drug I had discovered. I chose to try one. Within two months, I was taking over 40 of these little demonic explosives a day. I was eating half of them and injecting the rest into my veins. Yes, the little demon got me. I was becoming so addicted to this powerful drug that I remained high for three years without ever coming off the drug. I learned to live my life so engulfed in drugs and alcohol that I couldn't even think. I would sit in the corner for days at a time and never speak a word. I had become the worst person I knew. I was my worst enemy, but I didn't care. All that mattered to me was where and when I would get my next fix. Alcohol and drugs controlled my life. I was somewhere I never imagined I could be, an alcoholic, a drug dealer and user and a loser!

There were times when I was so stoned, I failed to remember where I lived or even who I lived with. Nothing was of concern to me. I didn't know if my children were being fed or even being cared for. I thank my God again for keeping watch over them when I chose not to. He and Peggy are the ones who kept them alive.

This was a bend in the road and I couldn't figure out how I had come upon it. I had definitely made some unfortunate decisions in my life but I still had no one to blame other than myself. By now, I was drinking beer, wine and whiskey; smoking cigarettes, marijuana and crank; eating and firing up LSD and speed wherever I could find a spare vein, and all from exploring the depths of my uncle's cabinets back when I was eight years old. Bad choices! Are you seeing the picture yet?

Meth

I remember the instant result, the first time I tested this drug. It was a different feeling, an almost instant feeling, a feeling that would change my actions, thinking, and my life for the next ten years. I recall the feeling of fear as this drug began running through my body. It was as though I should be afraid, but all I could think about was trying it just one more time. I could not recall any other drug making me feel so strong, but yet so weak; so smart, but yet so stupid; so powerful, yet so powerless. There was something about this new discovery that intrigued me, something that I wanted to drift away from, but I couldn't. I began begging for this new drug. All that mattered to me was finding someone, somewhere, willing to sell me any amount of meth. It was the first drug that I would steal from anyone around me, anyone who was as addicted as me. My manners and my charisma, what little I had, were disappearing. Friends weren't as important as they used to be. Meth was the most important thing to me. My wife, children, job, friends– nothing mattered any longer. Thinking back, I honestly believe that this was the only drug for which I would have killed another individual. I was so hooked on this little crystal demon that nothing in the world mattered any longer. I began to lie and cheat. I started stealing and cleaning the dropped coins out from beneath my car seats. I began to put this white powdery substance ahead of everything else in my life.

One thing I do remember is how terribly cold the floor would be as I sat in a corner for three to five days. I remember friends and sometimes even my wife and kids pouring liquid in my mouth and forcing food in me when they would find me so I would stay alive. The air would be hot one moment and the next moment I would be freezing. I recall driving and it seemed that the front of my vehicle stretched out nearly a mile. Street lights were lined

CHOOSE FREEDOM:
THE JOURNEY

up in a row, resembling other autos heading towards me. One night, I was driving down an interstate with cars passing me and coming towards me. I suddenly seemed to be riding on a child's ride at an amusement park. I pulled to the side of the highway, got out of the ride and began to walk around the car, trying to find someone to buy a ticket from so I could ride again.

Pulling up to a stop light was like watching a laser light show at the science fair, watching the trees blow and actually seeing the wind grab hold of the branches and pull and push them. I saw little green demons crawling all over the hood of my car, forcing me to go faster so the air would blow them away.

This new drug was ruining my mind. I seemed to be stronger than I ever was, so I used my strength to pick up something, anything, and destroy it. It didn't matter if I was at my home or someone else's home. It seemed my mind would focus on something and then convince me I had power over it and all I wanted to do was destroy it, just like this drug was destroying me! This went on for nearly ten years. I wanted to stop using meth, but I couldn't. I was becoming poor and more destructive. I would cry each time I shot this demon into my blood because I knew what was ahead and the thought made me tremble with fear. I was growing so tired of this drug, but every time I thought I could quit, some more found its way into my hands. Someone would come along or I would find a packet that I had hidden. Of all the drugs I did, meth was the worst! There were bragging rights for whoever could do the most at one time and stay high the longest. During days of being high, I thought that if I had just said NO the first time my so-called friend offered meth to me, I might not have felt like the loser I knew I was. Whenever you allow something as demonic as this to enter into your life, the drug becomes the winner and you are the loser, and that is exactly what I was!

Yes, it took me nearly ten years to distance myself from this addiction. Occasionally, after this episode came to a close, I would find meth in my path. I never could fully stay away from this drug; it always found a way to attract me! Today, it still amazes me that meth didn't show me to my death. So many times it would cause me to dream terrible dreams and think terrible thoughts, but I am so happy today that it didn't do to me what I witnessed it do to others. I've seen many lives destroyed by meth. These were terrible situations and I can only hope and pray that when you are offered this white explosive, you will say NO! (www.SayNOtoMeth.com)

Cocaine

Right when I felt my world was at an end, a new discovery came into my life. Was this finally the break I had been waiting for? The opportunity of a lifetime, I felt, had just been introduced to me–cocaine, the rich man's drug. Finally a drug that was enticing to many white-collar people as well as blue-collar. Opportunity was knocking at my door. Should I let it in? Yes, without a doubt. It was time for me to make a correct decision regarding the future of my family and me. We were finally on our way down easy street.

I was in my early thirties when this new discovery was made. My children had been around long enough to get to know me. I had spent enough time with them to teach them how to roll a joint and not to inhale so much as to choke. I had taught them how to weigh a pound of cocaine and not to allow their friends into certain rooms of our house. My two children knew to be quiet when bill collectors came to the door and not to answer the telephone unless it was late at night. They were receiving an education beyond imagination. They were both becoming young graduates from the school of hard knocks. I was proud of my family, not realizing they were so disgusted with me. Peggy always made sure there was food on their plates and her family always made sure she had the food. I didn't have time for family matters such as eating; I was busy planning our retirement, our future, becoming a sick drug dealer.

As I look back on years of my life, I realize more that I was an extremist at everything I did. Often times I was an extremist at things I didn't do. Everything I chose to do back then and still even now, I did to extremes. The cocaine venture I was being introduced to proved this. All of a sudden, without warning, I had become acquainted with an individual who was as sick as I was. He would buy nuclear waste drums full of cocaine from Peru, two at a time. We would work into the night preparing the shipment for distribution.

Dealing with this rich man's drug created new and exciting opportunities.

CHOOSE FREEDOM:
THE JOURNEY

I found myself being invited to parties given by prosecuting attorneys, judges, business owners and even policemen–those who were outstanding in the community and heroes in the face of the public. Dealing this new drug of choice became a nightmare. Money was more important than life itself. Gain was everything, loss was nothing. Even the loss of human life had become less important to me.

Alcohol and drugs had become my life. Something that I had decided earlier not to allow happen was happening. Why was it happening? Who was to blame? When would it end? These are questions I lived with for over 20 years. Why couldn't I come up with an answer? Could it have been that I knew the answer, I just wasn't willing to admit it? Was the world full of excuses that didn't apply to my life? What was happening to the seven-year-old who had welcomed a visit from a man named Jesus? What was going on? Do you know yet?

Chapter 12
Sad Corners Ahead

Now we come to the part of our journey where I will be sharing some sad and disturbing events, some events that I created and some in which I played a small role. The life I chose to live included many unfortunate and disturbing sights. Events that could and would only occur in a life filled with poison and demons. There have been times in my life when I was allowed to experience death and destruction. I remember when I took my first drink, I do not recall any warning signs in regards to what I was about to share. On the outside, so many things in life seem so beautiful, but on the inside, they are so disgustingly ugly.

Some of the more disgusting and sad happenings that occurred during my journey are these.

I witnessed early on, two twin brothers sharing a drug together and one of them overdosing in his brother's arms, watching the needle fall to the ground.

I witnessed a friend of mine shooting his own brother's jaw off with a rifle and then shooting him in the back of the head to finish killing him. He died at my feet and his blood stained my shoes.

I remember a best friend falling out in front of an oncoming vehicle on a main highway after leaving one of my parties; another best friend taking LSD for the first time and crashing his car into a wall, ending his own life. he was only 22 years old.

A twelve-year-old boy jumped from a third-story window feeling he could fly because someone slipped a pill in his pop; a friend's wife attempted to jump from a moving vehicle and the van rolling over her, leaving a husband

CHOOSE FREEDOM:
THE JOURNEY

and two young babies behind.

There were many more sad occurrences during my life of drugs and alcohol, but I choose not to mention all of them. Only enough to paint a black picture on the life and people I was involved with. A few of them are still in prison and a majority of them have never changed. If you are one of them and have reached this point in the book, please keep reading. You are about to discover what I found out and I hope you will choose as I did.

Chapter 13
Suicide was the Only Answer

I chose to live this worthless lifestyle until the age of 38. During those challenging years, I overdosed twice and lost everything I had except my family. I had been introduced to every drug known to man. I had become so addicted to alcohol that it was impossible for me to get drunk or high.

I recall the day I decided I was finished. I realized that I had made too many wrong choices and it was time for me to quit. Not time to quit using, but time for me to quit living. Yes, suicide. I set out one morning, 18 years ago, to kill myself. This is how it began:

I woke up that dreary morning here in Oregon and realized I never had hangovers any longer. I refer to Oregon because if you were in my family or knew me at all, you would have witnessed all of the moves that I made. I moved my family back and forth across the country at least five times, thousands of miles. I would try to settle us in one area and as soon as I would mess up, we would move again. One year my son Robert attended five different schools.

I lay in bed that suicidal morning and pondered ways to stop the lifestyle I had chosen to live. I had just received an eviction notice in the mail from our landlord and disposed of it in the trash. No one could tell me what to do any longer. I was a man and I wanted to flaunt my authority. I decided that morning that I had spent too many years hurting my family, my friends, and even complete strangers. I wasn't concerned about myself. It was time to put that hurt back on me, not understanding how much I was already hurting.

It was my day off, so I told Peggy I needed to go to the store after

52

CHOOSE FREEDOM:
THE JOURNEY

cigarettes. I took what money we had left and drove to the grocery store, the one I knew was next to the liquor store. I went in, bought cigarettes and a two-liter bottle of cola. I then went next door and purchased a fifth of whiskey. I poured half the cola out and refilled it with the whiskey. I decided that morning I was going to drink myself to death. I had marijuana in one pocket, cocaine in another and a bit of heroin I had stolen from a friend. I was going to ease the pain by hurrying it up.

I pulled away and started my drive to the Oregon coast. Something about the beach I admired and still do. It seemed I could always find God near the ocean. It hadn't dawned in me that I was searching for Him that day, but deep inside I knew He was the only one who hadn't given up on me, yet.

By the time I reached the ocean, I had drank the first fifth I had mixed, one hour, that was all the time I needed to drink what used to take me days. As soon as I found another liquor store, I purchased another fifth of poison, but this time I poured it into my windshield washer container. I had the cleaner hose running under my dash and that allowed me to push my washer switch and it would dispense a large amount of whisky into my can of pop. I was pretty proud of that idea and bragged about it to everyone. At least I could get rid of the bottle and not be caught with an open container. I also picked up two six-packs of beer. I needed a chaser.

I located the campsite where my sister and her family were camping, a few hours later. While I was waiting for their return, I found a cooler next to their camper. I opened the cooler and discovered a large bottle of champagne. Well this was a special occasion to me, so I popped the cork and enjoyed every drop. After I finished celebrating alone, I walked around the campsites and found a couple sitting enjoying a beer and they asked me to join them. After sitting and inhaling most all they had to offer, I said goodbye and returned to my sister's campsite. She required I eat supper with the family and after eating, we enjoyed drinking two more bottles of wine. Finally it was time for bed and as they retired to their camper, I decided to go on one last search for more drugs.

I remember treading up and down the beach. What exactly was I searching for on the ocean shore at 2 a.m. in the morning, all alone? I recall the sounds of families and couples sitting around their campsites and enjoying stories and songs, laughing and shouting, doing simple things that I began to dream of doing the same, someday, somehow, if I could only live. Instead, I was stumbling around confused, lost, hopeless and ashamed. What was the king of destiny, genius of time, the friend of the world, doing all alone on such a beautiful, sparkling summer night? I will never forget that feeling of loneliness. I kept walking and searching for answers. I remember the moon shining directly overhead as I stood a toe's distance away from the cold tide washing in.

I stared into the heavens and screamed, "God, are you anywhere near? Can you see and hear me? If so, would you please come to my rescue? I am so worn out and tired of living the life I have. I do not know what to do any longer. Please, help me, I am tired and alone, I give up."

Not fully understanding what I had just done, I walked on. I found a couple sitting by a fire with a cooler full of beer. They allowed me to sit and share their treasure with them and after it was gone I decided it was time to find my way back to camp.

It was now 4 a.m.. My sister left a sleeping bag out on the ground for me. I remember lying on the ground and staring towards the heavens again. What was up there that I was searching for? As I gazed into the sky, I realized I was not drunk and I was still alive. The accomplishments of the day were flashing through my mind. I began to add up the results and remembered that I had drank two fifths of whiskey, five six-packs of beer, two bottles of wine, one bottle of champagne. In addition, I had consumed one ounce of cocaine, one-half ounce of marijuana, a bit of heroin, not to forget over four packs of cigarettes and a couple of cheap cigars.

As I lay and prayed and tried desperately to transfer my soul into the heavens I was staring into, I knew I had consumed enough poison in one day to poison an entire crowd of people. Why was I still alive? What had gone wrong? Another foolproof plan had failed. Is that what the remainder of my life was going to be, failure? I also thought about my wife and children at home, again not knowing where I was and if I were alive or not. It was the first time in my life that I could remember feeling totally lost. My life had zipped by and the choices I had made had gotten me nowhere. I couldn't even die. What was happening to me? I began to cry and I cried myself to sleep that lonely night in the sand.

Chapter 14
Feeling a Change

I will never be able to erase the events that transpired the following day. It was August 6, 1987, a day that would go down in history as my first day on the road to recovery. I awoke to the sound of breakfast sizzling on the stove deep in the galley of my sister's camper. The ocean was pounding and children were up flying their kites and running about in the sand. For some reason, everything sounded and smelled so clean and clear, everything seemed different. I remember the kids popping out and seeming to welcome the presence of Uncle Donny one more time. I was always their favorite and I never could understand why. Maybe in their little minds there was a ray of hope for someone they cared for more than I did. It seemed back then that others knew me better than I did.

Those were the days when even children could sense my world crashing in on me. As I jumped up to greet the kids, I remember stopping and realizing that I did not even have a hangover and I didn't need to vomit. I was required to have a hangover with all the fresh poison circulating through my worn-out veins. Where had it all gone? Why wasn't I sick or hung-over? Why was my morning entertaining thoughts of sunshine and hope? Why was I beginning to feel concerned about my wife and children, whom I knew must be sitting at home wondering where I was this time and if I would ever return home?

Something was going on in my life that morning and I didn't understand it for years to come. The mirror I was staring in that morning was not illuminating what was behind me but what was ahead of me. How? What was going on? As the day passed, I began to acknowledge why this was

DON L. SUTTON

happening to me. The God that had His precious hands over me during all the failures and heartaches was about to do it again. He was the reason I was unable to poison myself that day. He was the reason I was still alive. God had never given up on me as I was approaching a time of surrendering of my own.

As I sat and shared the events the following day with my dear sister Debbie (whom Mom had taken away from me when we were kids), I recall the conversation we had that morning. She loved me so much and was so concerned for my safety. She was interested in my well-being and she did her best to reach out to me. Her main concern that morning, was if I knew what all I had done the previous day. I admitted I did and she began to lecture me as no one had ever done before, except Peggy. Peggy always lectured me but she was far away that morning as I began to reach out for help. You must finally reach a point in your life when you are ready to admit you are sick and that you want help. Once you decide to ask for help, you have admitted you have a problem and that you are ready for a change. Not until you admit it will you ever be able to change.

Debbie told me she was afraid for me and she didn't want me to die. Her life had been empty enough, as well. She and our brother Mike had been separated from Dennis and me and there was a time when my mom was too sick to care for them and they were put in a foster home. I still remember the horrifying stories about that home.

Little did Debbie know, the day before I had a plan for suicide. She asked me if I knew there were people and treatment centers that could help me if only I would ask. Right then I flashed back to the previous week at home. Never before had I seen so many commercials on television advertising a treatment center for alcoholics and drug addicts in Seaside, Oregon. Was this a coincidence or maybe the God I had been praying to the night before really heard me? I couldn't recall where the home for the sick was located, but it didn't matter. I wasn't ready for help; besides I still didn't think it existed or had I completely admitted I had a problem with anything. I had chosen for so long not to help myself, so what gave me the right to think anyone else could help me?

As we continued our conversation, she described a treatment center just up the highway from where we were and she told me the name was Serenity

56

CHOOSE FREEDOM:
THE JOURNEY

by the Sea. That was the center advertised on the television all week. Was this really happening? Why were so many different things beginning to have meaning, all at once? It had never happened before.

Rest Area

As we continue on our journey, I must stop here and explain something. There have been situations when I wasn't able to admit what I am prepared to share with you. Often in AA meetings and church meetings, I have not been allowed to express what I am about to explain. This is as perfect a time as ever. I know without a shadow of doubt that the last day that I drank alcohol and used drugs was the day that I cried out so loud to my God for Healing and deliverance and He heard me and healed me of a lifetime of destruction. I know it has been said that I have been in recovery, but I am entirely convinced that my most merciful God made a choice of His own that night when I was so sick. He reached those nail-scarred hands down on me one more time and touched my oh-so-sick body. I know this because ever since that night I searched for Him and cried out to Him on that lonely beach shore, I have not had one urge or desire for a drink or a drug. I receive my healing from Him and today, 18 years later, I thank Him and praise His wonderful name for hearing me and delivering me from over 20 horrible years of abuse and addiction to a world of sin.

Yes, I do believe Alcoholic Anonymous helped me and that they help others, but the higher power they encouraged me to believe in is the same God I saw in that little bathroom window that day and His name is Jesus. I worked the 12 Steps of Alcoholics Anonymous and I still carry their tools in my tool box. I use them nearly every day. Without Alcoholics Anonymous, it would have been much more difficult to find the answers to what was happening to me. I will always be grateful to AA for all it did and I will always be a friend of Bill's. I still have many friends involved in AA and I continually encourage them to keep going back. It works!

Chapter 15
A New Road Ahead

Well, I told Debbie and the kids goodbye and I began my long and lonely trip home. I was scheduled for work in just a few hours. As I walked away I reached in my pocket and pulled out the remainder of my fortune. One dollar left to my name. I had no banking account and nothing of value except for the three people sitting at home hurting. One less dollar and I would be completely broke. I left the campground and as I pulled out onto the highway, I decided it was time to start dreaming up another lie to tell my wife and kids as I was hurrying home.

I recall arriving at the intersection where I was faced with yet another decision. A right turn would send me on my way home and a left turn would send me in the direction of the treatment center I had been hearing about so much lately, another major choice to make. I decided, I turned right towards home. Suddenly, without explanation, I turned completely around in the highway and at once I was heading in the opposite direction. I was now traveling in the direction of Serenity by the Sea, the treatment center that had been the focus of my last few days.

I still do not remember turning that car around, but I will never forget it happening. I arrived in the small quaint village on the ocean edge in a few short minutes. I, by no means, put forth any effort to search for this retreat for the sick. I recall driving up and down a few short streets and ending up on a dead-end facing out across the that huge body of water, the Pacific Ocean. I turned my engine off and sat there, confused even more.

Staring out towards the horizon I began to realize how incredibly small I

CHOOSE FREEDOM:
THE JOURNEY

really was. I sat in awe and began to recite the Lord's Prayer out loud, that little prayer that stuck with me all of my life. After the ending and the echo of Amen in my ears, I started my engine again and backed up.

As I pulled forward to turn around, there it was. The biggest and brightest little dull sign I had ever seen. It read, Serenity by the Sea. I had been sitting in front of the retreat the entire time, all through the prayer I had just been praying. Was this a sign or just another coincidence? At that point, I was growing real tired of mistakes and things just happening. I pulled straight ahead, turned my engine off again, took a deep breath and marched right inside the front door. I was on a mission to prove my Peggy and everyone else wrong.

To end up where I was, I had made somewhere around five correct choices. Something was happening and I wasn't sure what it was. I hadn't made that many correct choices in the last year. Somehow the choices I was making seemed to be all the right ones. I had been delivered right to the front door of somewhere I had decided against, somewhere I had never been. During those times I knew absolutely nothing about AA. I always thought AA stood for Alcoholics Association. I had never needed help, or so I always felt. All I wanted from this visit was free information and a little encouragement. That would be a good excuse to offer my wife and children. I could really expound on this one. I wasn't there for memberships or titles, I was just in search of something and I knew not what. I needed help and I was finally realizing it. Could it be possible?

Chapter 16
My First Real Battle

I threw my tired shoulders back, opened the front door and charged right into the treatment center. Once inside, for some reason unknown to me at the time, I felt at home. Suddenly I found myself in the midst of others whom I felt I already knew. Some seemed to have hope in their eyes, others seemed as lost as I was, but I didn't care. I was there for me and no one else. After entering, I looked around and a tall gentleman approached me and introduced himself to me. His name was John Brebner. He was a tall, stern-looking man with hope sparkling in his eyes and a look of concern. I will never forget that look or that man.

As he approached me, I asked him if I could speak to the boss.

He stared through the toughness of my voice and replied, "We do not have a boss. I am the treatment director here and brother, you need help!"

How could he know that so soon? Who told on me? I didn't know one person there, so how was he able to see the hurt inside of me?

So I came right out and asked him, "How do you know that, sir?"

"I have seen many like you."

"Can you help me?" I asked.

"Do you want help?"

"I asked you, could you help me?" I barked back.

Again he asked, "Do you want help?"

Right then I knew I had to make another decision that could affect the outcome of my life. How do I answer this most important question? Was I in search of aid or was I just wasting time again? I must decide now for it was

60

CHOOSE FREEDOM:
THE JOURNEY

too obvious this old guy had met others like me before.

So I said, "YES I want help."

"Then we can help you," he replied.

Wow, that was one of the shortest and toughest battles I had ever been in and I wasn't sure who had walked away the winner. It didn't really matter. All that mattered then was that I get this visit over with and get back on the road towards home; I had to be at work in less than four hours.

He walked me into the office and we began to talk. He asked if I had insurance and I showed him my card. He took it from my hand and carried it into another office. When he left, I noticed all these positive attitude posters on the walls. I was already a positive individual and I didn't need any help in that field. I sat there and tried to understand what was going on. I was sitting in a place where I had never been and I was discussing my life with someone I had never met before. Plus, I hadn't had a drink all morning and didn't even want one. Something was wrong but, I couldn't put my finger on it.

John walked back in and sat at the desk across from me. He stared into my soul and immediately said, "Brother, you are in treatment!"

I jumped to my feet, grabbed my card and started for the door. He shouted at me and asked where I was going. I told him about my wife and kids who did not know that I was even alive and I told him about the job I had to report to in just a short time. I had no money or clothes with me and it was time to go. Suddenly I was hearing myself begin to make up for the correct decisions I was responsible for earlier that day. Suddenly without warning, I was back to my old self again and I didn't like it.

John stood up and spoke directly to my heart. "Brother, if you walk out that door, you will never walk back in another one."

That statement had a tremendous impact to it. I took a moment to dissect this final remark and I decided maybe John knew what he was talking about. I also began to cry like a baby. I pondered a moment or two and then admitted the reason I was there. This man saw right through me. I was impressed. He didn't back down from me like so many others had done before.

I stood silently for a few more moments and stared back into those worn-out looking eyes of John's. John had been where I was and he wanted to help me. He was serious about helping me and it seemed as though he really cared for me, and that was new. Did God place him there especially for me or was this another coincidence?

It didn't take John long to notice the tears rolling off my cheeks. There I was standing eye to eye with a man whom I felt was trying to reach into my innermost being and give me some assistance. I could feel the warmth in his eyes and feel the softness of his heart. He wasn't demanding; he just wanted to help me, after all that is why I was there. Finally he took control and summoned a man to take me and get me something to eat. He saw I was dirty and he could tell that I was hungry.

John assured me he would call my wife and my employer as to relieve me of those obligations. I, once more, reached into my depths and pulled out my white flag and surrendered. I had lost and won all in the same decision. This would be the beginning of my real journey. A foggy day at the beach filled with correct choices and a dim beam of hope. I was in a treatment center filled with other sick people like me. This would be interesting. Could there possibly be other individuals who had experienced a lifetime of total turmoil as I had? Were there others who had been mistreated? Were there other families, as mine, who had done without so many lifetime requirements? I decided then that I was going to discover every possibility regarding the unanswered questions I had been packing around all my life. I was going to make the best of this adventure. I wasn't leaving without answers.

Treatment was challenging! I was not prepared for what was about to take place in my life. I was on a new avenue full of new and challenging discoveries. But, I was armed and ready, armed with the grace of God and ready for direction. Any direction would be more rewarding than where I have been all my life. There is an old saying in AA and it explained where I had arrived in my life: "I was sick and tired of being sick and tired." I also knew, that day 18 years ago, that the God who had not lifted His hands from me through all the storms in my life wasn't going to dump me now. I was there for a reason and I knew God was the reason.

I later discovered that nearly everyone who came to treatment, especially those as sick as I was, were required to spend up to a week in detox. This

CHOOSE FREEDOM:
THE JOURNEY

was a room where some were even required to be strapped in straightjackets and they would lay and scream while the alcohol and drugs were leaving their systems. The doctor never could understand why I wasn't required a stay in that sickening little room, but later on in life, I understood.

Chapter 17
I Found my Sanity

Well, sanity was at hand. I was faced with learning how to be organized and being given lessons in discipline. I remember the first day, after being welcomed by all the other addicts; I was given an ashtray, a coffee cup and a napkin ring. Confusing at first, but eventually these three little inexpensive items would become a major part of my treatment. These three items were all I was allowed to have with me at all times. I was to be held responsible for knowing their whereabouts at all times. If I, for any reason, left even one of these articles unattended, someone would snatch it up and I would be required to sing five songs in order to gain possession of them again. I realized this was to try and teach me responsibility, and it did. I sang more the first week than I ever sang before. You would think as many times as my cup became hostage; I would have become an opera star. No, I just began to concentrate more on the reason I was required to follow orders.

Another event I recall was Teddy Bear Tuesday. This also was confusing at first, but eventually it became big part of my recovery. Every Tuesday we would be required to pick a teddy bear from a box and this bear was your mate the entire day. They came in different sizes and if you were one of the more fortunate ones, you could capture the smaller ones first. This fuzzy little companion had to be with you everywhere you went and teddy bear abandonment really costs you. When this act of abandonment occurred, you were required to sing seven songs and an apology to regain custody. These immature rules seemed so childish and trivial at first, but after I began to

CHOOSE FREEDOM:
THE JOURNEY

realize the importance of responsibility, I began to look forward to Tuesdays and I reached for the biggest bear in the box. There really was meaning to this childish act.

I was in treatment for 33 days. Looking back, it still amazes me the amount of discipline I received during such a short period of time. I seemed to be discovering more about myself in this worn-out old beach home than all the stops I had ever made my entire life. Was there something special about this place or had something taken place deep within me that I hadn't uncovered yet? I soon would find out as I was continually searching. I felt better about myself than I ever remembered and I was going to discover why. Life was beginning to matter and what few things I had managed to hold onto were also becoming more meaningful to me. This was something I thought I could learn to like, but it was growing on me, fast!

While in treatment, I met many others challenged with the same problems that I was facing. I was amazed when I discovered that some of these sick people had been in other treatment centers. Why? How could anyone who had bottomed out, as I did, ever want to return to the life they were retreating from? How, after a few days of learning you could still survive without poison traveling through your veins, could anyone return to that lifestyle again? It wasn't too much longer until I decided the reason for someone wanting to relapse. As I watched others struggling as I was to understand why we were all so much alike, I determined right away that was so true. And as I continued researching my so-called disease, I began to understand why we were all there and why some were in their second and third treatment centers.

As I remember back, I am reminded of an influential, older gentleman, I met at an AA meeting while I was in treatment. After quite a lengthy meeting one Saturday night, he came over to me and told me he could see my desire and willingness to stay clean and sober.

He shared this with me. "Son, you always remember this: Ask God every day, the rest of your life, for help and thank Him every day as well."

He shared a cliché with me that I have never forgotten and have quoted to myself nearly every day for the past 18 years: "Yesterday is history and tomorrow is a mystery. Today is a gift, that's why they call it the present."

This old guy had been clean and sober for over 40 years. That little bit of advice has remained with me for over 18 years. It seemed to be one of those tools I received while I was deciding to rebuild a new life. I took with me every tool that anyone had offered me. When I began this treatment process, my toolbox was empty. Today it remains full and to this day I use each tool when the need arises!

I realized after a few days that some of the residents who were there seeking help were already convinced they would use again. I met many who had all the answers for everyone else; they just didn't know how to apply them to their own lives. There were some who were very educated and some who weren't. Some who knew much and some who knew very little. The only thing we all knew and had in common was that our lives had been a total mess. Being educated and regimented meant nothing. Alcohol had no choice of whom it would choose and devour; it would and could attack anyone. I had witnessed this for the past 30 years. I also witnessed much denial in so many others; those who chose not to admit they were sick and chose not to seek help.

I remember a young man named Bill. He was a nice-looking young man and this was his third treatment program. Looking back he just wasn't ready to quit. He did, however, complete this program. One night when we were sitting in the big room, Bill called a meeting on me. He insisted to everyone that I was convinced that I was going to whip this problem I had. We all began to discuss how we were going to get through life and each one of us was led to talk about out higher powers. When it came to me, I chose to refer to my higher power as God, the one I saw in that little bathroom when I was seven years old.

When Bill was asked about his higher power, he referred to the light bulb which was hanging over the top of us. Later that evening I asked Bill about his so-called God and if he was going to take it with him.

He said yes.

Then I asked him what he would do when it burned out.

He told me the bulb was a god and it wouldn't burn out!

Well, we got out of treatment the same day. I would see Bill at the Aftercare meetings each week, and every Tuesday he seemed to be doing better. Then one Tuesday he was missing from the meeting. The next week we learned that Bill had gotten a job, a new little apartment downtown and his parents found him lying in the bathtub with a syringe still in his arm.

CHOOSE FREEDOM:
THE JOURNEY

Myself and another friend from treatment attended Bill's funeral and I have always wondered where that light bulb was when Bill needed it, that so-called god of his. It was probably broken and shattered in the dump somewhere!

As I settled into this program, I was beginning to find some answers to problems I had been facing. It seemed as though all the answers to so many different problems were the same. The answers to most problems were simple. I had made too many wrong choices, choices that if I had made differently would not have turned into problems. I was beginning to understand the real reason I was there.

I first was instructed to memorize the first three steps of AA. As I write each one, I would encourage you to try and understand as I do. They are so simple and are so easy to understand.

We admitted we were powerless over alcohol.

Now that was a simple statement, or was it? Maybe it was difficult to admit powerlessness. Maybe it was difficult for me and you to admit anything. It was always easier to admit something someone else agreed to rather than putting it on us. We were too busy trying to escape from admitting anything. I know why this is the first step. If you can agree to this step, the other steps seem to fall into place.

We came to believe that a power greater than ourselves could restore us to sanity.

There was that word power again. What was so important about this little word? Then I decided. I was on a power trip most of my life. And one thing for sure, when it came to saying NO, I was powerless. But how could any power restore me to anything? It must have more meaning than I was hearing. And how could anyone even suggest I had lost my sanity? That added new meaning to this step. I was insane and didn't even realize it.

We made a decision to turn our will and our life over to the care of God as we understand Him.

There it was! Finally the answer I was looking for. The God who continued to watch over me and hear my cries for so many years, was the reason I was there. That was the decision I had made a few days earlier. It was true. His hands had guided me along the rugged paths I had staggered down. Here He was, right where He led me. From this step forward, treatment became real.

DON L. SUTTON

The next few weeks were filled with new and exciting adventures. Discovery also played an important role in learning. I discovered more sick individuals coming in and out of my life. I witnessed some leaving the center and going out into the world with a fresh start and some going out on their own, individuals who should not have been there in the first place. They were the people who weren't ready for change and they knew it.

I, however, was not one of them. It was only a short time until I began to notice the fresh smell of the air. I began to hear sounds as never before and I began to see things I never knew existed, things like, sunsets and rain, wind and stillness, laughter and tears, light as well as darkness, laughter and silence, but most of all peace and serenity. I was becoming acquainted with sights and sounds that always have been a part of my life but I was too sick to recognize them, blinded and deafened by my poison!

So, here I was. I found a retreat, right on the beach in the great Pacific Northwest. Housing and food included, for one price. What a price I had paid for 33 days of luxury. Over 25 years of torment and disaster; many nights filled with heartache and sorrow. Was this a time for me to feel sorry for all the wrong choices? Could I search deep enough into my past to find the real reasons for a life of sin and shame? Would I finally be able to choose from a list of reasons and excuses why I had been a failure for so many years? My answer was NO!

I began to see my life more seriously than ever before. It was time for me to find the real reason for all the bad decisions I had made for the past 30 years. Yes, I sometimes had used many excuses for the things I done, but I did not want to use them any longer. The fact was that I was surrounded by many new acquaintances who seemed to have a desire to accompany me on my road to survival.

Everyone put forth so much effort to convince me that I was actually worth something. No one in my life ever recognized that trait in me before, except for my Peggy, Robby and Becky. Could it be right for me to think of myself as being worth anything? After all, I spent most of my life accepting opinions from others that were just the opposite. The scars that family and friends left on me indicated to me that I was nothing and never would be! How could I possibly be worth anything after being used and abused by so many for so long? How could anyone who did not know me have the authority to even

CHOOSE FREEDOM:
THE JOURNEY

try to convince me that I, Don Sutton, was worth even another chance?

This puzzled me at first, but the more I was reminded, the easier it was to accept. Maybe what they were telling me was true and I had made the wrong choice to allow opinion by others. I, after only 33 days, was being convinced by a group of alcoholics and heroin addicts that I really was worth something after all. I was beginning to understand why they were trying to convince me of this, and I needed to convince myself. I must admit it took a while, but now looking back, it was one of the most important issues in my life. Finally, I am worth it!

Chapter 18
A New Life Begins

Finally I was also realizing that it really was possible to survive without drugs in my system, a life with my family, my job, my friends and even myself without a desire to run out and get drunk or high. This seemed impossible at first, but as the days drifted by, I began to believe in myself and I was beginning to enjoy the feelings of real meaning which were bubbling up inside me. I finally understood the word peace and I liked what it stood for. Who was this new person I was meeting? Why hadn't I met him before? Why did I allow everything to happen to him? Why didn't I ever allow myself to meet me?

Life was beginning to be fun and I was attaching my inner being to every new experience that came along. Some of these new experiences were milk with my meal, going to bed before morning, watching the sunrise and set, feeling the wind blow and watching the trees sway. I also recall for the first time in my life, falling on my knees and thanking God for something rather than asking Him for everything. I could feel the change in my life happening. I could never remember waking up in the morning and being proud of who I was and where I was. I was beginning to adapt to this new lifestyle and I liked it a lot!

Often the memories of others would drift back into my mind. Many said I had a disease, others referred to my sickness as being hereditary and others blamed it on my genes. Some called it a habit while others described it as stress related. Which excuse applied to me?

As for disease, why weren't they giving us medication other than what we

CHOOSE FREEDOM:
THE JOURNEY

had gotten sick on? Why did I never hear of cures for my so-called disease? I was always assured there was no cure, so why try to find one? What about the monies organizations were collecting for research?

As for my sickness being hereditary, why wasn't anyone else in my family, as far back as I can remember, never as sick as me? Somewhere, someone surely would have been traced forward to me. No one I had ever known, so that trashed this theory. This was, without a doubt, the most difficult excuse for me to understand.

As for habit, yes, I could accept that one. You need not be a rocket scientist to come to that conclusion. This I could accept. It not only applied to me but it applied to every other human being on the planet. Finally, I decided I had acquired a bad habit and it was time for me to do something about it.

The conclusion I arrived at was this. I decided to turn myself in for treatment for a habit I had acquired somewhere back in my life. I had chosen to be where I was for one reason and one reason only, Don Sutton. I spent a lifetime trying to please others, never caring to please myself. I had dropped my world in on a situation where I felt I could find some reason to my being. And I wasn't leaving until I got some answers.

This program I became institutionalized in wasn't so bad after all; it was the first time I could ever remember doing anything and having no desire to have a drink to get me through it. I decided right away I was there and I was staying there until I discovered what I was all about. For once in my life, I was ready to surrender to anyone who I felt had a solution. I began to follow the instruction of my peers and I began gathering every tool they were willing to offer.

I learned to follow direction well and within 33 days, I was faced with one of the hardest choices I had ever made. I had to walk back out that door I had marched through so torn apart only days before. Yes, back out into that world that had always delivered me so many tough blows, a world where reminders and temptation lurked around every corner. Everywhere I would turn, my past would be there waiting to grab right back onto me. Was I ready? Could I do it? Would I do it?

The choice was mine. All of the lessons I learned for the past 33 days and I was still being faced with decisions. Was I finally ready to make some right choices or would I choose to return another time? No! I was sick and tired of being sick and tired and I wasn't coming back. My mind was made up, no turning back now. I was a new creature and I had to prove it and I had grown accustomed to this God I met so long ago.

Well, I went home and as the days passed by, I felt as though I was a time bomb to some and to others I felt as though I had a disease that if anyone touched me it would spread throughout the land, just like leprosy. Seemed as though everyone one was waiting for me to blow up or die!

My wife and children treated me as if I were a newborn in need of love. I must admit, I welcomed this treatment. When beer commercials would appear on our television, the kids were quick with distractions and finding the remote. They would direct me away from the beer aisles in the grocery stores and cringe as we passed a liquor store. Very seldom was there any mention of my past. They wanted to forget the terrible road we had been on together. I knew in their hearts there was a void waiting to be filled; a brand-new life for our family was all they desired and a new dad whom they had been dreaming of and waiting for, literally all their lives. A new hope for their future! Finally a dad and husband they need not be ashamed of. Someone they could hold worthy in their hearts. A real live person!

After treatment, I continued to attend AA meetings. I worked their program as they recommended. I attended aftercare for months and I made it to 90 meetings in 90 days. I had decided to give it my all and that is what I was doing. I had come too far and my family was watching and depending on me not to fail. I was so blessed to still have my family. Most everyone else in treatment wasn't as fortunate. I did not want to lose what my wife and children had struggled so hard and long to gain–togetherness, a family!!

I must admit this. My God; my wife Peggy; the treatment center, Serenity by the Sea; the treatment director, John Brebner, and my counselor Gary Brebner; were five of the most important influences in my recovery. God was my healer, Peggy was my hope, the center was my shelter, and John and his son Gary were my builders.

This was an opportunity God gave me to find others who were as sick as me. It was an opportunity He gave me to finally find someone who had proven solutions to a problem I had been facing for most of my life. I was

CHOOSE FREEDOM:
THE JOURNEY

given a chance to come together with a group of individuals who were able to understand the disruption that had plagued me for so long. I didn't need to be concerned that some educated professor, who had never experienced the things that had hurt me for so long, was dissecting me. I never had to worry about long lectures or instruction about what had been clinging onto me for so many years. I was allowed to sit and share with others who had been in some of the same frightening corners where I had been and real people who had been hurt and abused as I had. Finally, I discovered that I was not alone any longer and many others were facing the same problems I was faced with. It was up to us, as individuals, to decide the approach we each must take to stay alive.

Well, we are getting closer to the end of our journey together. Again I must explain the reason of our journey thus far. I am not proud or boastful regarding all the bad choices I have made in my life. I want you to understand that I have shared this portion of my life with you only to disclose the possibility that you have made some of the wrong choices which I have. I have a difficult time understanding how professors and scholars, doctors and lawyers, can come up with so many conclusions about life's most complicating events without ever having experienced them. Those were always the ones I never wanted to listen to; they couldn't possibly know what I was going through because they had never experienced it. My desire is to convince you that I am not one who can only speculate. I have been where you have been or perhaps where you are right now, or even where you are headed and it was not fun!

As we continue on towards the real reason for this journey together, I ask that you accept my discovery with an open mind and an open heart. I have accomplished only what you can as well. I have been there and I am not going back. Please understand the simplicity of recovery. Most miss the point because it is so simple. Please believe!

Chapter 19
The Real Reason

As I have struggled through my journey and looked back on all of the good and bad times I endured, and if all the years could be summed up in one word, it would be choice, not excuses. Traveling back through my life, sorting through all of the excuses I used to live the way I did, they could no longer have any validity. The things that family and friends had done to me during my adolescence were still nestled in the memories of my mind. But, I am not drinking or using. Why can't I drink now or get high on drugs? Why am I not abusing myself and others the way I used to; the excuses are still there for the taking? Why have I begun to make different choices, not the same as I made once before?

I have confirmed during my journey back, that excuses are like dreams; everybody has one. Dreams are more of a challenge and without excuses your dreams are more likely to come true!

Actually all the effort and tears that I shed over the past three years writing this book, was to discover the real reason that I lived the life that I did then and now, and to be able to share my discovery with you, hoping that you could and would make the same discovery, before it is too late. Here is my discovery:

Choice. Such a small, yet powerful word, that we all must come to terms with, over and over in life, often times choosing to face the challenge, other times without a choice. The importance of this word can seem so trivial, but it can and will change everything we encounter in life. It can change the future!

For those who do not wish to admit any form of powerlessness, the result

CHOOSE FREEDOM:
THE JOURNEY

can definitely be disaster. Those who do realize powerlessness, and think before they choose, can overcome and experience victory. It's usually up to you!

The dictionary's definition of this powerful word: choice–the act of choosing; power of choosing (there is that word power again); care in selecting; suggests the opportunity or privilege of choosing freely...choice. Such a small word yet powerful enough to change the world, and large enough to change your life.

Since the beginning of time, choices have been required. Did God choose to create this world we live in? Did He choose to make man in His own image? Was it Eve who made the wrong choice to eat from the tree of life and then allowed Adam to make another wrong choice and eat it as well, only to affect every form and issue of mankind since? Did David make a right choice to slay the giant; and Moses, was his choice correct to obey God? Did Noah make a good choice to obey God as well before the rain started? Do presidents and royalty always make the right choice when it comes to law and war? Have your parents or peers always made the right choices for you or themselves? Have the children in your life made bad or wrong choices? Do you choose to accept these beliefs and decisions? Get the point yet?

Allow me to reminisce a bit about my Peggy and me. When we were young and dating, I remember going out on Saturday nights. At the burger house, we only had to choose if we wanted cheese on our burger or not, only four different types of soda pop, weather to eat inside or outside, then if we should go to the movie or not. There were three theatres and each one advertised only one or two movies. And there was only one way to pay for the entertainment–cash. Even in high school we were not allowed a choice of what classes we would take. There weren't any to choose from. The choice was already made. You just didn't have too many choices to make. Simplicity. It seemed as though things were already decided, unlike today. Go to a hamburger stand and the drive-up lanes gets congested because those ordering just can't decide what they want. There are so many movie theaters now, each showing as many as 20 movies and decisions on what to watch are still hard. Choices on classes in schools now require a debate from the entire family.

DON L. SUTTON

We are faced with so many choices in our life. Everywhere we turn there are choices to be made. We often find ourselves choosing if we should make a choice or not.

I remember the first time I was offered a beer, the first time I was offered a drug, the first time I had an opportunity to tell the truth or lie. I can remember the first time that I was confronted with stealing or even giving, even the first time I was being sexually molested and decided to choose to keep quiet, when I had to decide to stay home or leave! Every time I was faced with good or bad events in my life, I was forced to make a choice, right or wrong it was made and my destiny followed.

So many times, as I look back, the choices that I made were wrong. Yes, I made a few right choices, but they seemed to always be more important. The wrong choices I made seemed to be harmless and trivial, yet they are the ones that destroyed my well-being for so many years of my life and nearly cost me my family!

Could it be as simple as this? Two little words, yes and no. They surely couldn't have been the cause of me losing most of my life to pain and defeat. Something bigger than this had to be the reason I was afraid and alone, but what was it? Yes, that is the conclusion I have come up with, I lived my life the way I did because I chose to. No one else was to blame and no other reason or excuse was needed. I did it because I wanted to!

This is the real reason that I have spent so many months, weeks, days and hours, taking this journey back in time, sitting and crying as I faced those terribly wrong decisions I made. Having to dry the tears off of my keyboard and wiping my eyes to continue my quest to try and understand what went wrong and what really caused me to waste so many years of my life; searching desperately to find the exact point where I had lost my self-respect and dignity; reliving all the nights I stayed out and all the pain I caused my family and the families of others; all the money and time I spent alone; all the people I chose to distribute my own poison to and the distance I put between me and my two children, my wife and everyone else who cared for me: It was my choice!

I made the choice and my family and friends were forced to suffer along with me. I was suffering right along with everyone, but I chose not to care. I chose to inflict the pain and sorrow I had stored up in my mind on me and

76

CHOOSE FREEDOM:
THE JOURNEY

everyone close to me, and it was wrong!

Looking back on all the years I drank, I do not recall anyone ever holding me down and pouring alcohol in my body. Never did anyone hold me hostage and force me to stick a needle in my veins and inject poison right into my blood. I was never forced to do anything I have written about. I was the one who chose to spend most of my paycheck on the way home. I chose where I would stop to drink and then I would choose what I would drink. Most times I was alone, so there was no one to assist me with my choice.

I lived the lifestyle I lived because I wanted to; I thought I was having fun. The life I lived was not because I had a disease or someone in my family passed it down to me, it was a choice and only a choice that I made!

And as well, the lifestyle I am living now and have been for the past 18 years has been by choice also. All of the temptations that used to haunt me are still there. Often I admit there are now more temptations in this world than ever before. There are more taverns, more brands and types of alcohol, more drugs and even more lust stops. There are more reasons for divorce and as many perverted decisions to be made than ever before. However, as the lists get longer, there still remains only two choices, those two little words, yes and no. And along with only two choices comes only one chooser, and that would be me! I could get in my car, drive to a bar, and sit and drink for hours. I could spend every dime I have and lose everything I own, but today I choose not to!

Chapter 20
My Eyes Began to Open

Are you seeing the possibility for you to stop what you are doing and begin to make some right choices? Wouldn't it be nice if staying clean and sober could be this simple? Well, it is and I am a perfect example of this. I am not a professor or scholar who has never experienced what you or someone you know is experiencing. I am a very common individual, who by the grace of God is still very much alive.

Can you decide that it is up to you? Do you want what I obtained so easily?

If so, take the first step; admit it. You are powerless over alcohol and drugs and your life is unmanageable. You are powerless over people, places and things.

Do something about it. Make a choice right now! Do not allow anyone to wound you or do with you what they want to do. Realize when to say yes or no. Admit that you are worth it and always know that you are. Speak up, do not carry a set of torn luggage with you through life, you deserve the best! And always remember, "If anyone is worth it, you are!"

I know you are ready to welcome in change. This welcome mat is lying out waiting for your first footprint. Wipe the dirt off your soul and be clean. Leave that bottle or drug sitting on the shelf and stay sober. Take the first step. Don't let anyone push you or pull you or you will just fall. Get rid of the denial and admit you have a problem, it is so obvious. Denial is not a river in Egypt. Learn to live your new life one day at a time. Do it yourself and the second step will follow; now it is your choice!

Conclusion

I know there will be some who will disagree with my finding and they have the right to make that choice.

Please understand, I am not trying to prove anyone wrong. I am just sharing a journey that began in the dark, and has ended in the light. I realize there are many who will accept the choices of others and some who will not and that is okay. I want you to always know that you will always have the right to choose. But please remember this: if the choices you are making or have made in the past are not proving to help, try not to make another wrong one; think before you choose.

As I have discovered, I made a lot of choices and until this one and most of them were wrong. The choice I made over 18 years ago is the only choice that made a positive change in me and everyone around me. The morning I pulled that little white flag out of my soul and began to wave it certainly indicated I was ready to surrender. Aren't you ready to start waving your white flag of surrender?

I am so glad I listened to my heart and turned to God for guidance. God continues to guide me down the right path. Yes, I continue to stumble and fall, but He is always there to help me up, just as before. I spent most of my life proving to myself that when I tried to do things my way, I failed. Now my life is different and I never want to return to that life again and I never will; I truly believe that. Yes I still stumble but not as often, I have learned to walk one step at a time, one day at a time. I have gained my self-respect and my dignity back. I now have more than any one man deserves, and I am so proud of all my accomplishments.

DON L. SUTTON

At first it wasn't as easy as it is now. My Peggy tells me it took her nearly five years before she knew when I walked out the front door, I would return. My children have seen me in the light over half their lives now. I have a ten-year-old grandson, Anthony, who never has had to see a side of Grandpa that would have saddened him or caused him to make bad choices. I have another grandson, Samuel, and a granddaughter, Olivia, who will both grow up to remember their grandpa as one of the greatest men who ever lived. I am blessed with a son-in-law, Wayne, and daughter-in-law, Kimberly, who will never be forced to feel sad with their mates because of something their father did to hurt or embarrass them.

Oh, if you could only feel the love I have for God, my family, my friends and life in general and, I am so happy to be the person that I am now and as I look at myself, I see that all the scars have disappeared. They are gone and I choose to never allow them to return and fester.

As I continue to read my road map everyday, my Bible, I am taken back to one of my favorite verses. The book of Galatians, chapter 5, verse 1: "It is for Freedom that Christ has set us Free. Stand firm, then, and do not let yourselves be burdened again by a yoke of slavery."

That yoke has been torn loose and tossed away, never to fit again! I will always refuse to choose to allow my past or present to hang loosely around my neck. The yoke I once wore will never entangle me again, yet the choice I have made to live today will be worn proudly on me every day for everyone to see. I hold my head up high with absolutely nothing to fear or be ashamed of. I am so happy to be the person who I am and I hope you will make a choice to share that feeling with me!

So, I pray you have enjoyed this journey back through my life. I hope you have discovered something on this journey that can and will apply to you or someone you know and love. It has been very difficult for me to relive some of the events in my life. I suffered much agony while writing, as it took nearly three years for me to complete this trip for us.

I have forgiven all who tried to or did harm to me. My family has forgiven me for all the wrong choices I made and most of all, God has forgiven me. Once I forgave myself, it seemed as though everyone else followed suit; try it!

I must thank my father, my wife's mom and dad, Curtis and Freida for all

CHOOSE FREEDOM:
THE JOURNEY

their prayers for me. My sweet mother-in-law has said a prayer for me every day for over 40 years. I couldn't have made it without them! I want to thank my Peggy, Robby and Becky for believing in me and never giving up. God is my foundation now and my family is my shelter. When I was in need, they were there and they still cling to a hope they knew existed.

And thank you for taking this journey back with me. My prayer is that you never get as sick as I use to be. Chances are you could be less fortunate! If you do choose to stay sick, take this road again sometime and maybe you will find that one of the broken paths or one of the intersections we encountered together along the way will change your direction. After all, if the direction you are going is getting you nowhere, turn around! Don't continue to fight the hills; learn to enjoy the valleys. Strive to climb, don't settle for less. You only have one shot at this life, so live it to the fullest and do your best. Stop using the past to ruin the present. Do not depend on others; allow them to depend on you. Be who you want to be, not what someone else wants you to be; go for the gold don't settle for the silver; stand strong and always know that you are worth it!

God bless you! I pray that this journey has been a worthwhile trip for you. I hope I have made it as clear as possible and allowed you to cross all the bad spots with me. Who knows, maybe someday we will cross paths again, I can only hope.

Your friend, Don

Notes from the Kids

I felt my journey back was complete, but I have something more I was asked to share with you. When I thought I was finished with my story, I printed copies of my completed manuscript and gave copies to my two children, Robert and Rebecca. I asked them each to read what I have shared with you and then for them to be open with me and critique my work.

Robert was the first one to read and he gave me his approval. He told me he found it interesting and a little difficult to read. He remembered more than I shared, but there were some things we wanted to keep to ourselves.

Rebecca called me the following morning and was crying as she shared her

DON L. SUTTON

feelings with me. She suggested I write this portion of the book and share with you some of the reasons why and how I left scars on my kids. She felt it necessary to share some of her pain with you, hoping maybe it will convince you not to involve your children, or any children, in the type of lifestyle that nearly tore our family apart.

Rebecca shared some events with me, which quite frankly, I never knew existed. Here are some things from my kids that they hope will give you more understanding about how we affect those we love, more than we ever know.

Becky wrote:

One of the first memories of the lifestyle my dad instilled in my innocent mind was during my kindergarten year. Daddy always told me to never tell my teacher what we do at home or we will all be in trouble. I knew all the trips my dad was taking and I remember him teaching my brother and me how to roll joints and take short puffs, as not to choke. I was six years old and had already had more experience with drugs than any child deserved.

I remember always making geographical moves and without any choices, changing places to live and starting new schools. I would just begin to make new friends and then we would get kicked out and have to move somewhere else. My confidence and self-esteem were beginning to diminish with the moves.

Then the third grade. I remember the house where we lived. It was the nicest house we ever lived in. Dad's drug business must have been improving. That was the house where Dad began to allow Robby and me to fill shot glasses with beer. The glasses were small, but never a mention on how many of them we were allowed to consume. For me, there weren't many,. I hated the taste of that poison.

Another memory from that house was during one of my dad's parties, I was sleeping in my bed and a friend of Dad's brought a girl into my room and began to have sex with her, in my bed. They thought I was sleeping, but I was laying there scared to death!

There was either something about that house or some reason why I remember so many evil things about it. I remember the evening Dad had a New Year's Eve party and one of the couples in attendance began to argue. The young man was too high and he walked out of the party. The following

CHOOSE FREEDOM:
THE JOURNEY

morning we received word that he had fallen on the highway and was run over by a vehicle. He was a good friend of Dad's but that didn't slow him down. Life didn't seem to matter to him–only alcohol and drugs.

The last memory I have of that year was when we received word that Daddy had been in a fight and was taken to the hospital, really hurt. When Mom took us up to see him the following day, I remember how bad his face was scarred and bruised. We didn't even recognize him. He had been beaten by two men in a bar fight.

Then we got evicted from that house and moved a few blocks away. At first it seemed like it would be better. Dad had a pool table and pinball machine downstairs. Robby and I had fun whenever the parties weren't going on and that was very seldom.

That was when Dad decided to make me his own little bartender. He taught me to mix his drinks just the way he liked them. Little did he know that every time I was sent upstairs to mix him a drink, I spit in the drink as I was taking them to him. I mixed other drinks for his friends and I spit in every one of them. Because he seemed so proud of me for being his slave, he would allow me to play pinball during his parties. I remember how hard it was to follow the ball because of all the cocaine on top of the glass. Sometimes I thought about experimenting with the cocaine, but I was afraid I might die. I always wondered if that happened if Dad would miss me.

Mom began to join in on the parties, seemed she had to in order to spend time with Dad. They both stayed out until early in the morning. Robby would feed me and put me to bed. I have always believed that was why Rob and I were so close, and we still are. We were all each other had!

When Dad fed us, it was usually brownies with hashish in them, so it would make us sleepy. They wanted us asleep and out of the way.

Then we moved to a little house in the country. Dad's alcohol and drug use seemed to be getting worse. I don't think parents realize how much kids notice what is going on in the home, but if you love someone, you watch and care. Mom and Dad had a bad argument in that house and Dad left and took me with him. Dad left Mom and Robby with no food to eat. Her family brought groceries to the house so we wouldn't go hungry. The next move we made was clear across the country; we moved to Washington State.

Dad rented a nice house. It was so pretty on the outside, but inside it was total darkness. I remember after we moved, Dad had a friend and offered him money to move what we had to our new land. Dad never would send him the money he promised, so we lost everything we had. Everything I had accumulated in my life was somewhere in Montana, never to be seen again. I still wish I had some of the things I cherished, but they probably do not exist any longer.

Yes, a nice house and a red BMW in the garage, but no beds, no kitchen table and lawn chairs in the front room. On the outside Dad always looked good, but we always knew how ugly he was on the inside!

It wasn't long until we were evicted from that house and we moved to Oregon. Dad was always running from his responsibilities and commitments. We lost everything we had again and I was getting so tired of this lifestyle.

Now I was in the eighth grade. Why had life been so bad for so long? I began to grow tired of this lifestyle, so I sneaked a phone call to my grandparents. I cried as I explained to them all that had happened. They convinced my parents to allow them to fly us back to their house and they would take care of us. Dad convinced Mom it was the right thing, so we left them 2,000 miles behind. I remember Robby and me crying on the plane. We held hands and Rob assured me he would do his best to see that I wasn't harmed again. He told me we had each other and I still love him so much for all he did for me. He was my rock and I held on to him, he was my new dad at 14 years old.

We stayed a year with Grandma and Grandpa. After school was out, we moved back to Oregon. Mom and Dad sent Robby back to Grandma and Grandpa's to finish High school. I missed my rock; Dad was still drinking and getting worse.

By then I had decided to try smoking marijuana. After all, Dad had taught me how to smoke it. The marijuana seemed to relieve the peer pressure and I began to like it. That is when I began to sneak around and discover the effects of alcohol.

Shortly after Rob's graduation, he began to party with Dad. He just wanted to be around Dad, so he decided to do some of the things he witnessed Dad doing. We both wanted to be a part of our daddy's world, but in order to do that, we had to do what he did. Too bad he didn't like going to the park or to the zoo!

CHOOSE FREEDOM:
THE JOURNEY

I remember when Dad checked himself into treatment. Mom and we knew he was on another one of his trips and we never imagined a change was on the horizon. I remember Mom, Rob and I getting evicted from our house while Dad was healing. We were forced to move into an apartment. All we had to move in was an old four-door car, but we did it because we didn't have much to move.

We visited Dad at the treatment center and we began to notice a change in him. It seemed as though he really did want to change; well, so did I!

I began to drink and party more. It was as though I was trying to give him a taste of his own medicine. He had ruined me and I wanted him to pay for it. Yes, that was as good of on excuse as I needed. I could go out and do anything I wanted to do and blame it all on Dad.

Now my life has changed. I have an awesome husband and God gave me a gift like no other, a son. Because of the change Dad decided to make, our entire family has changed. We are all so close and love flows through our homes like never before. Anthony only knows his grandpa as his "best buddy in the world." Fortunately, Anthony has only experienced the light side of Dad, he will always know his grandpa for who he is now!

Dad's discovery is correct. As I became an adult, I had all the excuses I needed to live the way I did. I had been on a journey of my own, like no other. Looking back on my life, when I became of age, I decided to live my life the way I did, no one else. Just like today, I do what I do because I choose to.

It was difficult for me to write these stories. I wanted Dad to share with you the sick effect these lifestyles have on the family and especially the kids. I remember a whole lot more, but what I have shared will hopefully leave an impression in your mind. Kids see more than you think they do. They see all the bad things you do and they remember what they want to. Hopefully, because of my tears, you will stop what you are doing before you scar the ones you love.

I hope my dad's journey to freedom encourages you to get help. If you could only experience what I and my family are experiencing, you would never want to live the way we did. My dad tells everyone that if life was any better, there would have to be two of him, he couldn't stand it alone! Thank you, Beck.

Robby wrote:

When I approached Robby to write about bad times he remembered, he told me he chose to forget the past. He indicated to me that it really didn't matter to him what I did 20 years ago, all that mattered to him is what I do now.

He doesn't want his children, my grandchildren, to read or hear about my past. He wants Samuel and Olivia to only know me for who I am now; that is all that matters to him and his wife Kim.

I love and respect my dad and he is one of the major reasons I am who I am. I will always believe in him, Robby told me!

Dad wrote:

Isn't this another prime example of making choices? Some of us choose to accept things the way they were and others choose to accept things the way they are. The choice is totally up to you. That is exactly what this book is all about. Take what you have read and apply it to your every day living. Remember, "Think before you choose."

I want to take the time to thank my Peggy, Robert and Rebecca for helping me through this journey. I hope and pray that you use the examples I have set to continue to make right choices on your own journey. As we continue to travel through the rest of this life, let's all work together and help one another choose right. God bless each of you on your journey and always remember to give thanks where thanks is due
Dad

Proverbs, chapter 3, verses 5 and 6
"Trust in the Lord with all your heart and lean not on your own understanding: in all your ways acknowledge him, and he will make your paths straight."

The End

Printed in the United States
69113LVS00005B/454-471